Stephen R. Covey

6
EVENTS

EVENTS

THE
RESTORATION MODEL
FOR SOLVING
LIFE'S PROBLEMS

STEPHEN R. COVEY

DESERET
BOOK
SALT LAKE CITY, UTAH

Library of Congress Cataloging-in-Publication Data
Covey, Stephen R.
  Six events / by Stephen R. Covey.
     p. cm.
  Includes bibliographical references (p.   ) and index.
  ISBN 1-57345-187-8
  1. Christian life—Mormon authors. 2. Mormon Church—Doctrines.
3. Church of Jesus Christ of Latter-day Saints—Doctrines. I. Title.
  BX8656.C656 2004
  248.4'893—dc20
                                96-022574

Printed in the United States of America   72076
Publishers Printing, Salt Lake City, UT

10   9   8   7   6   5   4   3   2   1

To my grandfather Stephen L Richards,
whose concept of building
a gospel-centered, intergenerational family
has inspired me all my life

CONTENTS

Acknowledgments   ix

Preface   xiii

PART 1: THE LORD'S PROBLEM-SOLVING MODEL

1. The Challenges of Life   3

2. The Six Transcendent Events of the Restoration   13

3. Internalizing the Six Events: A Plan of Action   25

PART 2: THE SIX EVENTS

4. The First Event: The First Vision   35

5. The Second Event: The Restoration of the Gospel   73

6. The Third Event: The Restoration of the Priesthood   109

7. The Fourth Event: The Restoration of the Church   133

CONTENTS

8. The Fifth Event: The Restoration of the Keys of Salvation   161

9. The Sixth Event: The Restoration of the Temple Ordinances   187

PART 3: THE PERSONAL RESTORATION

10. The Significance of the Sequence   219

11. The Importance of Experiencing All Six Events   237

12. A Constant Renewal   245

     Bibliography   265

     Problem/Opportunity Index   267

     Index   271

ACKNOWLEDGMENTS

T HE SEQUENCING THEME HAS BEEN my fascination all of my adult life, but never as much as in this book on the six transcendent events of the Restoration. I've been working on this book off and on for more than twenty years and feel a deep sense of gratitude to many individuals who have encouraged or assisted me in one way or another. I'm grateful for the inspired teachings and testimonies of the Brethren and for their profound influence upon my entire life. I'm also grateful to the many, many people all over the world who have positively or negatively responded to presentations and who have given careful, thoughtful, caring feedback in order to make the material easier to grasp and stronger in its impact.

I am particularly grateful to the many people in different situations of life who have shared their stories describing the power that comes from the proper sequencing of their gospel experiences, as well as what happens when the sequence is violated. Many of these individuals were utterly at the "end of their tether."

I am very grateful for many friends and associates at Deseret

Book who have assisted in the editing, artwork, and production of this book. I am particularly grateful to Sheri Dew and Cory Maxwell for their confidence in the material and for their continual encouragement over several years to get this book out. Emily Watts has been a superb editor who wisely and carefully struggled with me to overcome my tendency to make the material too theoretical and too overwhelming. With great care and devotion, Andrew Allison provided invaluable editorial assistance in early drafting years ago, for which I am deeply grateful. I also express thanks for Jack Lyon's editorial expertise and Tonya Facemyer's excellent work with the typography. Working with the people at Deseret Book has also been a source of silent encouragement to make sure that the material is orthodox, mainstream, and authoritatively supported, particularly when viewing the Restoration through this rather new and different in-depth *sequence* angle.

I appreciate the artistic talent and empathic sensitivity that Scott Eggers has displayed in dealing with all of the visual elements of this material. His contribution has been tremendously important in making the material inviting and encouraging to the reader—particularly for people like myself who like to use their right brain as well as their left brain.

I'm grateful to Patti Pallat, Nancy Aldridge, Julie Judd Gillman, Marilyn Andrews, Diane Thompson, and Christie Brzezinski for the excellent, professional office help they have given. Heartfelt thanks also goes to Kathryn Daines Davis for organizing firesides for me to teach this material and for interviewing scores of people willing to share their inspiring stories. I also appreciate the able research assistance of Dr. Bruce Van Orden and my son Joshua, who, in the center of a high-pressure period just prior to his BYU graduation, took time to give me understanding regarding the conditions that the Lord established in preparation for the Restoration. My dear friend and professional colleague, Boyd Craig, who manages my various book projects, has been a constant source of organizational and leadership support, encouragement, feedback, and inspiration.

I am grateful beyond expression to my magnificent eternal companion, Sandra, and my entire family for their patience, understanding, and encouragement for the past two decades of this project. I'm sure they're sick of it by now, but they have just never said so. I thank also my dear sisters, Irene, Helen Jean, and Marilyn, and my brother, John, for their constant encouragement and support.

Finally, I acknowledge God's affirming hand with a profound sense of appreciation.

PREFACE

THIS IS THE FIRST BOOK IN MORE THAN twenty years that I have written specifically for members of The Church of Jesus Christ of Latter-day Saints. Although the principles it contains have a broader application, it focuses on the *sequence* of events unique to the restored gospel of Jesus Christ.

Many Latter-day Saints who are acquainted with my national-market books and seminars have expressed admiration for how I teach gospel principles in my professional work, as if I had some kind of hidden agenda. I always answer that I have no hidden agenda, that the principles I teach in those contexts can be found in all six major world religions. I make a sincere and sustained effort in all my professional writing and teaching to include nothing that is unique to my own religion. Basically, when I write to the world, I am teaching the universal, timeless, self-evident principles of integrity, kindness, service, fairness, continuous improvement, and so on. These principles, when lived, will lead any person or organization to greater effectiveness, peace, happiness, and contribution.

But many of the greatest challenges, deepest desires, and richest opportunities in life and *eternity* can never be met by these principles alone. These require more—principles, covenants, and ordinances on an entirely different level.

Let me give an illustration of the difference between universal principles and the higher ones I'm describing. You'll find that most of the writing and speaking that has deeply influenced people for good includes the ideas of taking responsibility, exercising initiative, and becoming the creative force of your own life. Ella Wheeler Wilcox put it this way: "There is no chance, no destiny, no fate, / Can circumvent or hinder or control / The firm resolve of a determined soul."

"Invictus," a poem by William Ernest Henley, sums up this theme in its last two lines: "I am the master of my fate: / I am the captain of my soul." In somewhat of a rebuttal to this idea, Elder Orson F. Whitney of the Council of the Twelve wrote a poem titled "The Soul's Captain." It opens with these lines: "Art thou in truth? Then what of Him / Who bought thee with his blood?" This poem teaches what the apostle Paul taught about the atoning sacrifice of Jesus Christ: that we are not our own, that we are "bought with a price" (1 Corinthians 7:23). Therefore, we should look to the Lord as the captain of our soul. Now, that is a higher level of teaching, a different level of understanding.

I'll juxtapose these two poems side by side. As you read them both over, you can begin to sense the difference. Look inside yourself to see what impact each of them has upon your mind and your heart and your spirit.

INVICTUS
by William Ernest Henley

Out of the night that covers me,
Black as the Pit from pole to pole,
I thank whatever gods may be
For my unconquerable soul.

In the fell clutch of circumstance
I have not winced nor cried aloud.
Under the bludgeonings of chance
My head is bloody, but unbowed.

Beyond this place of wrath and
*   tears*
Looms but the horror of the shade,
And yet the menace of the years
Finds, and shall find me, unafraid.

It matters not how strait the gate,
How charged with punishment the
*   scroll,*
I am the master of my fate:
I am the captain of my soul.

THE SOUL'S CAPTAIN
by Orson F. Whitney

Art thou in truth? Then what
*   of Him*
Who bought thee with His blood?
Who plunged into devouring seas
And snatched thee from the flood,

Who bore for all our fallen race
What none but Him could bear—
That God who died that man
*   might live*
And endless glory share.

Of what avail thy vaunted strength
Apart from His vast might?
Pray that His light may pierce the
*   gloom*
That thou mayest see aright.

Men are as bubbles on the wave,
As leaves upon the tree,
Thou, captain of thy soul! Forsooth,
Who gave that place to thee?

Free will is thine—free agency,
To wield for right or wrong;
But thou must answer unto Him
To whom all souls belong.

Bend to the dust that "head
*   unbowed,"*
Small part of life's great whole,
And see in Him and Him alone,
The captain of thy soul.

I do believe that the principles illustrated in "Invictus" can lead a person to the higher ones taught in "The Soul's Captain." As we read in Doctrine and Covenants 84:46–48, "The Spirit giveth light to every man that cometh into the world; and the Spirit enlighteneth every man through the world, that hearkeneth to the voice of the Spirit. And every one that hearkeneth to the voice of the Spirit cometh unto God, even the Father. *And the Father teacheth him of the covenant* which he has renewed and confirmed upon you" (emphasis added).

In this book I desire to go beyond the universal. I want to discuss ideas that can lead us to the kind of life that God and Christ live. I do so with respect for the many readers whose beliefs will differ from my own, but without apology for sharing as much as I can of concepts that have eternal consequences for our hearts and souls.

One note as we begin this journey together: I am convinced that different people learn things in different ways. I have included charts and illustrations in the book, for example, because I know that many people are visual learners. Many benefit from an organized plan of action, and one is offered in this book, but if that's not your style, don't worry. Apply these concepts to your life in the way that makes the most sense for you—there's not necessarily "one right way" to understand them. And remember, although there is an orderly sequence to these events in the way that they are presented here, they also intermingle and support each other all along the way. (The Holy Ghost, for instance, though discussed more completely in the third event, is an important presence in all the six events.) My greatest desire is that you will find ideas in these pages that will bless your life and your family.

PART 1

THE LORD'S PROBLEM-SOLVING MODEL

THE CHALLENGES OF LIFE

CHAPTER 1

THE CHALLENGES OF LIFE

CHANCES ARE, MANY OF THE people you see every day—those you work with, those you live with, those you care most about—are facing serious challenges. How many of the following people do you know?

- A divorced woman who struggles with her sense of self-worth.
- Parents who are trying to cope with the increasingly rebellious and alarming behavior of a teenage child.
- A teacher who is having trouble connecting with the class.
- A returned missionary who has lapsed into apathy about both the Church and life.
- A father who feels unhappy and unstable in his job.
- A young adult whose fear of the future has her paralyzed.
- A mother who feels overwhelmed with the demands of her small children.
- A married couple who just can't seem to communicate with each other.

Our mortal probation is a time of problems and challenges. It was meant to be so, as the Lord said, to "prove them herewith, to see if they will do all things whatsoever the Lord their God shall command them" (Abraham 3:25).

But our Father in Heaven, in his mercy, has given us patterns to help us overcome our trials in this life. I suggest that there are *three fundamental examples,* or models, given us by God that will help us in any situation. The first is his Son, Jesus Christ, our Savior and our Redeemer. He is the model for each of us personally in the development of our characters, our personalities, our whole lives. "I am the way, the truth, and the life," he taught. "No man cometh unto the Father, but by me" (John 14:6).

The second model is the *temple.* This is the model for our homes, filled with purpose, order, cleanliness, equality, reverence, love, and accountability. Home and family are the foundation of the Church and God's kingdom, both on earth and in heaven. The temple is the expression of the highest celestial culture found on this earth, a place where God himself comes. It is his house, his home, and a careful, prayerful analysis of the entire temple experience will reveal a thousand reasons why God has given it to us as a model to strive for, especially for those of us coming from broken homes, dysfunctional families, and single-parent realities.

The third model, the main subject of this book, is the restoration of the fullness of the gospel of Jesus Christ—our Heavenly Father's plan of life and salvation for his children. The key to understanding and internalizing the Restoration lies in the *sequence* of the six transcendent events that took place from 1820 to 1844. *Transcendent* in this case means superior to, absolutely necessary, supernally important, beyond comparison with anything else, and foundational to all other significant events. These six events provide a problem-solving model that is overwhelming in its beauty and effectiveness.

Our Heavenly Father's Challenge

The Restoration was the Lord's response to a very specific problem: His children all over the earth were in a state of immense darkness. Not only had they lost their way theologically, but this darkness pervaded every field of knowledge. By the early 1800s, the world had lost a complete and correct understanding of God, of Christ, and of man. The principles were changed, the ordinances had been counterfeited or lost, and the priesthood was no longer on the earth. The world was deeply mired in apostasy. Darkness covered the minds and the hearts of the people, to the extent that one part of this period of time was even called the "Dark Ages." Numerous creeds abounded, and yet millions of God's children were coming into the world with little chance or likelihood of ever finding the fullness of light and truth.

Elder Bruce R. McConkie wrote of this era, "Angels no longer ministered to their fellow beings; the voice of God was stilled, and man no longer saw the face of his Maker; gifts, signs, miracles, and all the special endowments enjoyed by the saints of old were no longer the common inheritance of those in whose hearts religious zeal was planted. . . . There were no legal administrators whose acts were binding on earth and in heaven. . . . The religion of the lowly Nazarene was nowhere to be found. All sects, parties, and denominations had gone astray. Satan rejoiced and his angels laughed. Such were the social and religious conditions of the day" ("Once or Twice in a Thousand Years," *Ensign,* November 1975, 15).

Now, think on God's purpose: to bring to pass the immortality and eternal life of man (see Moses 1:39). How would he accomplish this purpose in a world filled with such darkness and confusion? How could he bring light and knowledge to mankind in a way that would enable someone *without* this light and knowledge to gain access to it? We know that he loves us, and that he loves all people alike. No one is special in his sight, for he is "no respecter of persons" (Acts 10:34; Doctrine and Covenants [D&C] 1:35; 38:16). But in fact everyone is special in his sight, for "the worth of souls is great in the sight of God" (D&C 18:10).

In solving *the world's* problem, the Lord has shown us how to solve *ours,* because we face the same challenge he did—how to help those around us discover their true identity and fulfill their divine potential. He said he would show us "a pattern in all things" (D&C 52:14), and I believe that the pattern by which he restored light and truth to the earth is the perfect model by which we can restore light and truth to our own lives and to the lives of others, especially our children and those within our stewardships.

A New Paradigm for the World

Most of this book will focus on behavior, not doctrine or history, although the primary focus of the book will be on the events of the Restoration, which are historical and which teach doctrines. President Boyd K. Packer has taught that "true doctrine, understood, changes attitudes and behavior. The study of the doctrines of the gospel will improve behavior quicker than a study of behavior will improve behavior" ("Do Not Fear," *Ensign,* November 1986, 17).

Why is this so? Because all of our behavior is based upon our understanding of life. Change that understanding, and the behavior will change. For instance, to use an analogy, suppose you knew we were in the middle of a three-act play, in the act called "Mortality," with the first act being "Premortal Existence" and the third act "Life after Death." If you knew that your eternal progress was a product of your obedience to the laws and ordinances of the gospel, would this not shape your behavior in mortality, the "second act"? Of course it would. But if you thought that mortal life was the only act and that you were not accountable and there was no afterlife, would that not shape your behavior?

Science has a name for this. It's called "paradigm shifting." A paradigm is the theoretical explanation or model of the way things are. For instance, bloodletting was a practice in the Middle Ages, based on the paradigm that the bad stuff is in the blood and you need to get it out. When the germ theory was discovered—in other words, when the paradigm shifted through the discovery of germs—a new medical therapeutic model was adopted to reflect that understanding, that new paradigm.

Another example: Centuries ago, the earth was believed to be the center of the universe. When the sun was found to be at the center of the solar system, astronomy changed completely, which had an enormous impact on other fields of knowledge. You will find in the entire history of science and humankind that almost every significant breakthrough was a "breakwith"—a break with some traditional belief or doctrine or paradigm. As Albert Einstein taught, "The significant problems we face cannot be solved at the same level of thinking we were at when we created them." When paradigms shift, practices and behavior shift also.

We can easily understand the importance of having a correct paradigm by using the analogy of a *map*. If you were trying to find your way around Los Angeles by using a map of Chicago, and if that map were your only source of information, you'd be hopelessly lost. If someone told you to "try harder," you could double your speed, but you would simply get lost twice as fast, because you'd still be following a false map. After a while you would probably get discouraged and just quit in frustration.

Someone might see you looking dejected and say, "You've got an attitude problem. Be positive." So you could try to think more positively and start again. As a result, you'd be more cheerful, but you'd still be lost. The point is that your ability to reach your destination has far less to do with your attitude or behavior than with the accuracy of your map.

Truth itself is an accurate map of "things as they are, and as they were, and as they are to come" (D&C 93:24). True doctrine leads to accurate maps.

If you want to make small improvements in your life, change your behavior. Change your attitude. If you want to make quantum improvements, change your paradigm, your map. In other words, begin to look at life and the world from an entirely different level of thinking. Then and only then will behavior and attitude become important.

I've often shared how several years ago, I had an experience with a change in paradigm while riding to church one Sunday morning in a New York City subway. It was a fairly quiet ride until a father and his children entered our subway car. The children seemed completely undisciplined and unruly, and they violated the whole spirit of that calm, Sabbath morning. They were running around, jumping up and down, pulling people's newspapers down, and even purposely bumping into people. The father sat right next to me, put his head down, and didn't even try to control them. After waiting several minutes to see if he was going to do something about them, I turned to him and said, "Sir, don't you think you could handle your children a little better? They are upsetting a lot of people." He looked up as if he had just become aware of the problem, and then he said, "Oh, I know. I'm sorry. We have come from the hospital where my wife just died. I guess the kids don't quite know how to take it, and, frankly, I don't either."

Believe me, my paradigm of that whole situation shifted immediately and dramatically, and I suddenly desired with all my heart to help that family. Why? Because I now had a different map of the same reality—a map that was more accurate.

Now consider what might have happened if the paradigm shift had never occurred, if I had never found out what had really happened. I might have sat there, trying hard not to let the situation bother me, but inside getting more and more upset. Or, through a sense of embarrassment or annoyance, I might have felt obligated to "help" somehow, to make those children behave. In other words, I might have tried to force either my attitude or my behavior. But after the shift, I no longer had to "try" to change my attitude about the situation, and I no longer felt the need to make the children behave. My attitude and my behavior changed instantly, without forcing them in the slightest. I didn't have to "try harder." I didn't have to increase my willpower. The change emerged naturally from the new paradigm, from my new understanding of the situation.

Now, that is exactly what happened to the world through the Prophet Joseph Smith. "On the morning of a beautiful, clear day, early in the spring of eighteen hundred and twenty," came forth a single prayer from a young man who had been prepared for generations through his heritage to ask the deepest question that flowed from the deepest hunger of the soul (see Joseph Smith—History 1:14).

When he left the Sacred Grove, Joseph Smith understood the world differently from when he went in. He had a new map of reality. Because of his experience, he was beginning to understand who God was, who Christ was, and who he was. He learned a little about his role in life. He saw everything in a new light. That was the beginning. From that point on, looking through anything other than a celestial lens to understand the meaning and purpose of life would be like holding up a flashlight to get a better view of the sun.

After the First Vision, other events in the restoration of the gospel added more insight, more understanding, to the Prophet's new, true way of looking at the world, a way that had been lost to humanity for nearly two thousand years.

The accompanying chart shows Joseph Smith's work on a timeline that helps solidify the sequence of the events in our minds.

Life and Work of Joseph Smith

Palmyra, (Manchester)	Palmyra, (Manchester) Harmony, Pennsylvania	Harmony, Pennsylvania Kirtland, Ohio Far West, Missouri Nauvoo, Illinois
1805	1820	1830 1844
14 years—growing up	10 years—preparation • *First Vision* • *Moroni's visitation / Book of Mormon translated* • *Priesthood received*	14 years—establishing the kingdom • *Church organization* • *Keys of the priesthood* • *Temple ordinances* • *Sealed his testimony with his life*

THE SIX TRANSCENDENT EVENTS OF THE RESTORATION

THE SIX TRANSCENDENT EVENTS OF THE RESTORATION

To end the long night of darkness that had engulfed the world, the Lord set in motion the glorious latter-day Restoration. "It came about in a regular, normal process," wrote President Spencer W. Kimball:

> An inspired, fourteen-year-old boy had difficulty learning from the scriptures alone what the future was. In a dense grove of trees he sought the Lord and prayed for wisdom.
>
> The time had come, and though the adversary, Satan, recognizing all the powers of eternity which would be revealed with the gospel, did everything in his power to destroy the lad and destroy the prospects of the Restoration—in spite of him there came the splendid and magnificent vision to this pure, inquiring lad. Exerting all his powers, and with the strength of the Lord, the darkness was dispelled. Satan yielded and the vision proceeded, with a pillar of light coming exactly over the boy's

head—a light above the brightness of the sun, which gradually descended until it fell upon him. The young Joseph continues:

"It no sooner appeared than I found myself delivered from the enemy which held me bound. When the light rested upon me I saw two Personages, whose brightness and glory defy all description, standing above me in the air. One of them spake unto me, calling me by name and said, pointing to the other—This is My Beloved Son. Hear Him!" (JS—H 1:17.)

This formal introduction by the Father to the Son was most important, for this would be the world of Jesus Christ and the Church of Jesus Christ and the kingdom of Jesus Christ.

Questions were asked and answered, and eternal truths were given. It was made clear to the young, unspoiled Joseph that if he retained his worthiness and kept clean before the Lord, he would he responsible for the restoration of the Church and the gospel and the power and authority of God.

As maturity came to the young, unsullied man, there came also a flood, a deluge of ministrations from heaven. Commissions were given; authority was bestowed; information was given; and the revelations from on high continued almost without interruption, for the time had come. Conditions were ripe; many people were ready to receive the truth in its fulness.

In quick succession there came other visitors. Peter, James, and John—men who last held the keys of the kingdom, the power of the priesthood, and the blessings of eternity—appeared to the young man and restored the power and authority which they had held on earth.

John the Baptist, beheaded by Herod but now a resurrected being, returned to the earth and laid hands on the Prophet Joseph to give him the Aaronic Priesthood.

The great Moses of antiquity returned to the earth, a celestial being, and restored the keys of the gathering of Israel.

Elijah, the prophet of the eternal work for the dead, returned to make way and prepare for the great temple work and for the restoration of the gospel to those who had died without an opportunity to hear it.

The organizers of the Church were told by the Lord:

"No one shall be appointed to receive commandments and revelations in this church excepting my servant Joseph Smith, Jun., for he receiveth them even as Moses." (D&C 28:2.)

And the prophet Moroni appeared unto Joseph and spent long hours explaining the peopling of the American continents by the Lehites and also the Book of Mormon, which would be unearthed and translated. This book would be a further testimony of the coming of Christ to America and would give testimony that Jesus was the Christ, the Eternal God, for both Jew and gentile. This record, the Book of Mormon, would help to establish the divinity of the Lord Jesus Christ.

These were the beginnings of accomplishment; and the gospel was revealed, line upon line and precept upon precept, and truths were restored, and power was given and authority was revealed, and gradually enough light and enough people were there for the organization of this kingdom of God which Daniel saw two and a half millennia ago ("The Stone Cut without Hands," *Ensign,* May 1976, 9).

This grand system of Restoration can be broken down into six transcendent events:

The First Vision. In response to Joseph Smith's prayer for divine guidance, the Father and the Son appeared and spoke to him in the spring of 1820.

The restoration of the gospel in the form of the Book of Mormon. Several years later, the angel Moroni delivered the plates from which the Prophet Joseph translated the Book of Mormon—a new witness of Jesus Christ. It contains the fullness of the gospel, and its central message is Christ and his infinite atonement.

The restoration of the priesthood. Through angelic visitations, the Aaronic and Melchizedek orders of the priesthood were restored in 1829, making available the ordinances and covenants by which people can receive the blessings of Christ's gospel.

The restoration of the Church. In April 1830, God's kingdom was established again on the earth. For those who have entered into the covenant of baptism, the Church provides a support system of fellow believers, opportunities for personal growth through service, and a vehicle for taking the gospel to all who will receive it on both sides of the veil.

The restoration of the keys to save the living and the dead. In 1836, other angelic ministers restored the keys of authority required to fulfill the threefold mission of the Church: proclaiming the gospel, perfecting the Saints, and redeeming the dead. These keys and purposes give focus and direction to all of the work performed in the Lord's kingdom.

The restoration of the temple ordinances. After the way had been prepared by the first five events, the Lord revealed the sacred ordinances of the temple. This aspect of the Restoration was actually more a process than an event, taking place over a period of years in both Kirtland and Nauvoo. Because of these ordinances, eternal families can be created and our Heavenly Father's children can obtain the fullness of the blessings he has prepared for them.

Seven Foundational Questions

Through the six transcendent events of the Restoration, the Lord solved his problem of how to bring his children out of darkness. But in this book, we are striving to understand the *personal significance* of those events—that is, their power to change individual attitudes and behavior. I believe that these events answer seven foundational questions, each of which affects our capacity to fulfill our divine potential. The first six questions are connected to the six events we have already identified:

Who? Who is God? Who is Christ? Who am I? Who are you? The First Vision answers those identity and relationship questions. It shows us that we can believe what the Lord says about us—that he loves us so much that he sent his Only Begotten Son to redeem us (see John 3:16). That is the divine source of self-identification or self-definition—as opposed to the social source, which we are too often inclined to believe. The truth is, we are literally children of our Father in heaven, only one generation away. We are "of the Father."

Whose? Whose are we? To whom do we belong? Who paid the price? Who is the source of our salvation? The restoration of the gospel through the Book of Mormon stands with the Bible as another testament of Christ and clearly and plainly explains his role as our Savior and Redeemer through his infinite, atoning sacrifice. Thus it answers the question "Whose am I?" Clearly, we are the Lord's. As the apostle Paul wrote, "Know ye not that . . . ye are not your own? For ye are bought with a price" (1 Corinthians 6:19–20). Thus, we may say that we are "of the Son."

How? How do I get back to my God, my Father, my Creator? How can I become a partaker of the divine nature? The restoration of the priesthood suggests that we do so by receiving the ordinances of the priesthood by covenant, and these ordinances are the main vehicle in mortality for transferring divine energy and nature into our beings. These are far more than just social ordinances, for in them "the power of godliness is manifest" (D&C 84:20). This power is manifested by the Spirit, so we may also say that we are "of the Holy Ghost."

Where? Where do I go? Where can I find support, opportunity to serve, and direction for my life? These questions are answered by the restoration of the Church. We go to The Church of Jesus Christ of Latter-day Saints, which administers the *inclusive* plan of the Father to serve *all* of his children on both sides of the veil. By serving in the Church, we become sanctified as we leave our comfort zones, live outside ourselves, and come to unfold our true nature by living our lives for the Lord's sake. We receive as well the emotional and social nourishment of other people who are pressing along the same path. Thus the Holy Ghost is helping us to grow and develop and to more and more become "partakers of the divine nature" (2 Peter 1:4).

What? What do I do? What is my work in mortality? The restoration of the keys of salvation for the living and the dead shows that our work is the same as that of our Heavenly Father: "to bring to pass the immortality and eternal life" of all his children, our brothers and sisters (Moses 1:39). Our concern for salvation is comprehensive, *inclusive.* It embraces God's plan to save the entire human race—*all* of his children, living and dead. It helps us to see everything we have as a stewardship, whether it be our bodies, our children, our possessions, our time, our talents, or our opportunities.

Why? What's it all about? Why am I on earth? Why do I need to be married for time *and* eternity? The restoration of the temple ordinances answers the question of God's ultimate purpose. In the temple the new kingdom or the eternal family is created. As Adam and Eve were married by God for all eternity, so God's anointed priesthood holders marry or seal husband and wife for time and all eternity. In the temple we learn the answers to the most profound questions of life; we learn where we came from, why we are here, and where we are going. In the temple we are also instructed individually through the Holy Ghost.

When?—the seventh question—is answered in the *sequence* of the six events. If we want to use the Lord's problem-solving model successfully, this sequence is crucial. For example, if we try to get people into the Church before they understand the gospel, we violate the sequence. If we try to get them to the temple before they have been immersed in the order and work of the Church, we violate the sequence. It's like asking students to do calculus before they understand algebra. Whenever we violate the sequence, it can lead to serious problems later on that may be difficult to resolve.

The six events and their significance are outlined in the chart on the following pages.

The restored gospel is like a compass pointing north. The arrow on the compass is called the "direction of travel" arrow—in other words, it directs our values and our behavior. The Restoration revealed anew to God's children which way "north" is, and this came slowly, developmentally, and in proper order and sequence. It is now our responsibility to align our behavior, our attitudes, and our families with "true north," with correct doctrine.

The Six Transcendent Events of the Restoration

EVENT	DATE	PLACE
First Vision	Spring 1820	Manchester, New York
Restoration of the gospel through the Book of Mormon	September 1823– March 1829	Cumorah and Palmyra, New York
Restoration of the priesthood	May 15 1829; Late May 1829	Banks of the Susquehanna River, Pennsylvania and New York
Restoration of the Church	April 6, 1830	Peter Whitmer's farmhouse, Fayette, New York
Restoration of the keys	April 3, 1836	Kirtland Temple, Kirtland, Ohio
Restoration of temple ordinances	1836–1844	Kirtland, Ohio, and Nauvoo, Illinois

WHAT HAPPENED	PERSONAL SIGNIFICANCE
The Father and the Son appeared to Joseph Smith with messages	Identities and relationships (revelation) (WHO?)
Moroni revealed and later delivered plates from which the Book of Mormon was translated and published in 1829	The Model and the Way (Christ and the Atonement) (WHOSE?)
John the Baptist restored the Aaronic Priesthood; Peter, James, and John restored the Melchizedek Priesthood	Empowerment and the new birth (priesthood ordinances and covenants) (HOW?)
By revelation and law, the Church was officially organized by Joseph and five other priesthood holders	Support, order, and opportunity (WHERE?)
Christ, Moses, Elias, and Elijah appeared to Joseph and Oliver committing the keys of all dispensations	The keys, the mission, and direction (to save the living and the dead) (WHAT?)
A series of revelations through Joseph over an eight-year period	Eternal families; the fullness (WHY?)

This responsibility will not be easy. Just as a magnet can cause the needle on that compass to jump around, so does the power of disobedience and false tradition (see D&C 93:39), magnified by the popular culture of today, which is bent on distorting these doctrines, these paradigms, these divine models, and on calling evil "good" and good "evil." This is why we must pay the price slowly, patiently learning God's pattern, God's model, and God's sequence. Too often we're like fish that discover water last. We are so immersed in the element as to be unaware of it. We have eyes that do not see and hearts that do not comprehend. We need to pause, to stand away from and examine carefully this divine process—these magnificent, transcendent events of the Restoration.

The Lord's perfect problem-solving model can be used in any application, including parenting, teaching, missionary work, and even business. Think about how the Lord uses this pattern with his children, and then ask yourself, "Am I doing that with *my* children? Am I applying this perfect model in working with my spouse, my in-laws, my students, my ward members?" In other words, the way God solves problems with his own sons and daughters can become our frame of reference as we try to help the people we deeply care about. Consider how valuable that is—how infinitely valuable!

The Lord has given to us a perfect problem-solving model so brilliant in its design and so complete in its execution that any serious and sincere learner would feel overwhelmed, humbled, grateful beyond expression, full of praise and wonder and awe and humility and softness and openness.

INTERNALIZING THE SIX EVENTS: A PLAN OF ACTION

INTERNALIZING THE SIX EVENTS: A PLAN OF ACTION

ARLY IN HIS MINISTRY, THE SAVIOR TAUGHT, "My doctrine is not mine, but his that sent me. If any man will *do* his will, he shall know of the doctrine, whether it be of God, or whether I speak of myself" (John 7:16–17; emphasis added). In other words, to internally *know* is to *do* his will. To learn and not to do is really not to learn. To know and not to do is really not to know. We experience in the doing. Consider a sport, like tennis: We may intellectually understand the game, but until we play it (doing, experiencing), we don't really know it.

Understanding plus *doing* equals *internalizing.*

The purpose of this book is to encourage—hopefully even to inspire—each of us to regularly internalize the six transcendent events of the Restoration. They were external events to each of us. To internalize them, we will need to make them a part of our very being, our character. This, fundamentally, will come from our doing more than from our knowing, from our experiencing more than from intellectual understanding.

One of the most impressive character traits of the Prophet

Joseph Smith, which he exercised in every one of the six events, was his willingness to take initiative, to move out on his own in seeking, in knocking, in asking. We were made to act, not to be acted upon. Joseph Smith acted, and again and again the Lord responded. Similarly, when we act, we open the door for the Lord to guide us to further knowledge and understanding.

President Thomas S. Monson has said, "In this world in which we live, there is a tendency for us to describe needed change, required help, and desired relief with the familiar phrase, 'They ought to do something about this.' We fail to define the word *they.* I love the message, 'Let there be peace on earth, and let it begin with me.'" ("The Doorway of Love," *Ensign,* October 1996, 2).

How to Get the Most from This Book

One useful way to think about internalizing the Restoration and to seriously consider and adapt these principles to your circumstances is to look on doing so as a *one-year project,* with two months for each event. You might do this with your family, with a group of friends, with a fireside group, or just with yourself. Two months for each event would total twelve months. This would give you a sense of order and of sequence—which, I believe, is almost another word for order—and this may help you to have a sense of commitment and resolve. It would give you a sense of beginning with the end in mind, a sense of having a noble purpose or goal, a sense of accountability to yourself and to whomever you wish to be accountable for progress for the year. It would give you a sense of achievement, accomplishment, and progression, and this would encourage you to keep at it, to keep going.

You can begin your yearlong project anytime you wish. You

can even shorten it or lengthen it, as you choose. You may wish to read the entire book before you begin the process, or you may decide that you want to experience it as the Prophet Joseph did in its sequence, without an explicit awareness of all that will take place. You will know what is best for you and the approach you would like to take, but I would strongly encourage you to consider this yearlong process of devoting two months to each event.

As mentioned before, I've been working on this particular book for twenty years now and can testify of the power of the process, of the orderly sequence—of the power and significance of having a goal, a purpose, and a sense of progression and accountability, if only to yourself.

Three Common Mistakes

Before you begin, deeply consider the three problems or mistakes that are most common as people attempt to live gospel-centered lives. People who make these assumptions are not likely to succeed in internalizing the six events:

First, that *the sequence is unimportant.* Have you ever seen someone being pressured toward the Church before they understood the gospel? Have you ever seen someone being taught the gospel before they had any sense of their own worth and of your genuine caring for them?

Second, that *you don't need all six events;* you can ignore one or more of them. Have you ever seen someone who believed in Christ but felt that covenant-making and the ordinances weren't necessary? Do you really need to be involved in all three purposes of the Church: teaching the gospel, perfecting the Saints, and redeeming the dead?

Third, that *once through is sufficient.* Have you ever seen a returned missionary lose his or her faith? Have you ever seen a devoted priesthood leader, now released from a calling, replace fire and commitment with cynicism and anger?

Does this mean that a person needs to regularly go through each event slowly and patiently before moving on to the next one?

My answer is yes and no. Yes, in the sense that the first time should be in the proper sequence, just like our own temple experience for ourselves. No, in the sense that any of the events truly experienced and internalized always embody the earlier ones—just as when we do work for the dead in the temple, there are preparatory ordinances, endowments, and sealings. Furthermore, when we regularly internalize all six events, the nature of our insight and understanding of the first events is informed and matured by our understanding and insight of the latter events, so that it becomes almost like an upward spiral staircase wherein we experience these events in an entirely new way, with new meaning and learning. This is just as it is when we regularly worship and serve in the temple and when we regularly read, ponder, and pray about the scriptures.

Two Levels of Initiative

At the end of each of the chapters in the next section, I suggest two levels of action. This two-step approach will require you to exercise your own initiative, to step out as the Prophet Joseph did in bringing about the Restoration. The first level introduces basic, or personal, initiatives; the second represents a more advanced application that we will call "enlarging service initiatives." At the very end of the book, the entire list will be given, with space for you to mark your progress week by week on a scale of 1 to 5 for purposes of personal accountability.

A sports metaphor may reinforce the concept of how levels of development build upon each other. For instance, take a team sport like soccer. Until people are physically fit, they can't really develop the skills to play that specific game and to bond as a team. Similarly, in school, each grade builds upon the last one completed. We need to start at a basic level and then move forward into more advanced initiatives.

We are dealing with principles here, but we're also dealing with individual persons who have different levels of desire, commitment, patience, and skill, and who live in unique circumstances. The best way to get the most from this book is to figure out your own best way and adapt the suggestions to what you feel is most wise for you and your loved ones. Even though I will suggest that you seriously consider the two steps or levels of initiatives given at the end of each chapter, as the spirit of this process overtakes you, it will be like the spirit of conversion, and you will be guided by the inspiration of the Holy Spirit as to what else you should do next.

The following diagram suggests the cycle of learning that takes place as we commit ourselves to *do* what we are inspired to do. As it applies to this book, we might start in the center of the circle with one or two new concepts we have learned. Then, when we *commit* to act upon the knowledge we have gained, going forward and doing what we have committed to do, we learn even more, and we grow in our commitment to follow our *learning* with our behavior. Thus the cycle continues, and our knowledge and power to do grow ever larger.

Learn–Commit–Do Cycle

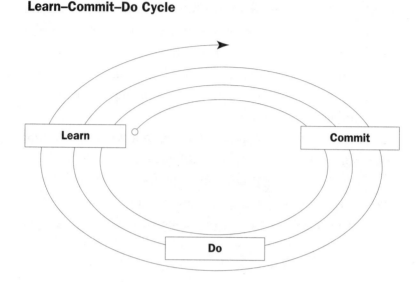

Learn by Teaching

Finally, I encourage you to consistently share or teach what you are learning. Everyone knows that *when you teach, you learn.* The Lord put it this way: "Teach ye diligently . . . that you may be instructed more perfectly" (D&C 88:78).

Teach your loved ones, teach your friends, teach anyone who might have an interest. Teach the personal significance of each event of the Restoration and the importance of the sequence model.

This teaching habit will deepen your own understanding and commitment to *do.* And when you acknowledge what *you yourself* are learning, it will both legitimatize and lubricate *your* changing and improving in two ways: first, as you teach in the spirit of humility, old labels you have placed on yourself will dissolve; and second, if you ask others to support and encourage you as you strive and struggle to live what you teach, you will form your own support group.

PART 2

THE SIX EVENTS

THE FIRST VISION

WHO IS GOD, AND WHO AM I?

CHAPTER 4

THE FIRST EVENT: THE FIRST VISION

WHO IS GOD, AND WHO AM I?

I BELIEVE THAT WHEN JOSEPH SMITH knelt to pray in a grove of trees in the spring of 1820, he was the voice of the entire world.

For centuries mankind had been striving to emerge from the Dark Ages. Their search for knowledge and self-awareness had led to the Renaissance, the Protestant Reformation, the establishment of a free nation in America, and the period known as the Enlightenment. Through prayer and Bible study, *many* sought for a greater understanding of God and his purposes.

Nevertheless, in the early 1800s most of the world believed deeply in a "worm theology," which defined man as a depraved creature, lower than the dust, whose highest purpose was to give praises to the Creator in this life and the next. In other words, people did not understand who they were. They had no concept of the eternal family, their true identity as literal children of God, their potential to become like our Heavenly Father, or the pathway that could unleash that potential.

In a real sense, the whole world was in darkness. As President Gordon B. Hinckley has said:

> Ignorance and evil enveloped the world, resulting in what is known as the Dark Ages. Isaiah had predicted: "Darkness shall cover the earth, and gross darkness the people" (Isaiah 60:2). For centuries, disease was rampant and poverty reigned. The Black Death killed some 50 million people during the 14th century. Was not this a season of terrible peril? I wonder how humanity survived.
>
> But somehow, in that long season of darkness, a candle was lighted. The age of Renaissance brought with it a flowering of learning, art, and science. There came a movement of bold and courageous men and women who looked heavenward in acknowledgment of God and His divine Son. We speak of it as the Reformation.
>
> And then, after many generations had walked the earth—so many of them in conflict, hatred, darkness, and evil—there arrived the great, new day of the Restoration. This glorious gospel was ushered in with the appearance of the Father and the Son to the boy Joseph. The dawn of the dispensation of the fulness of times rose upon the world. All of the good, the beautiful, the divine of all previous dispensations was restored in this most remarkable season. ("The Dawning of a Brighter Day," *Ensign*, May 2004, 81.)

When Joseph Smith entered the grove, he was unaware of his future role in the great latter-day Restoration; he merely wanted to resolve his confusion about which church to join. He believed and followed the counsel he had read in the New Testament: "If any of you lack wisdom, let him ask of God, that giveth to all men liberally, and upbraideth not; and it shall be given him" (James 1:5).

Events Leading to the First Vision

Before we examine the supernal significance of the First Vision, we need a deeper, larger perspective of the *divinely inspired* processes and events leading up to it. This long-term perspective will deepen our appreciation and humble us with a sacred feeling, a sense of stewardship.

Nothing was random or arbitrary about the Lord's choice to manifest himself to Joseph Smith. Men and women alike had been searching for truth long before Joseph entered the grove of trees, and his prayer to know the true Church represented similar prayers that had been spoken numberless times before him. Centuries before Joseph's birth, the Lord had started preparing the world for the restoration of the gospel. After the Great Apostasy swept across the face of the earth, the Lord guided a series of events that created the necessary conditions to set up his kingdom in the latter days. This process began with the social and intellectual revolutions of the Renaissance, Reformation, and Enlightenment, and consolidated with the colonization, independence, and political birth of America.

The Renaissance, a rebirth of classical culture and learning, began to loosen the chains that entrapped the darkened mind of man. Soon after, great men led a movement to reform the church and recover its original doctrines. Describing the period after the Dark Ages, President Gordon B. Hinckley writes:

> As the years continued . . . the sunlight of a new day began to break over the earth. It was the Renaissance, a

magnificent flowering of art, architecture, and literature. Reformers worked to change the church, notably such men as Luther, Melanchthon, Hus, Zwingli, and Tyndale. These were men of great courage, some of whom suffered cruel deaths because of their beliefs. Protestantism was born with its cry for reformation ("At the Summit of the Ages," *Ensign,* November 1999, 72.)

The Enlightenment followed, with its emphasis on breaking the intellectual bonds of authority and using one's own reason to discern truth. The motto of the Enlightenment became "Have courage to use your own understanding!" (Immanuel Kant, "An Answer to the Question: 'What is Enlightenment?'").

During the period of Renaissance and Reformation, an important event transpired that would further lay the groundwork for the Restoration—the discovery of the New World. Columbus's voyage was inspired by reasons other than mere adventure or glory, for the Spirit of the Lord came upon him. Notice the similarity of language used by Nephi—prophesying the discovery of America two thousand years before it happened—and Columbus:

And I looked and beheld a man among the Gentiles, who was separated from the seed of my brethren by the many waters; and I beheld the Spirit of God, that it came down and wrought upon the man; and he went forth upon the many waters, even unto the seed of my brethren, who were in the promised land (1 Nephi 13:12).

Our Lord unlocked my mind, sent me upon the sea, and gave me fire for the deed. Those who heard of my enterprise called it foolish, mocked me, and laughed. But who can doubt but that the Holy Ghost inspired me? (Quoted in Mark E. Petersen, *The Great Prologue,* 26).

Elder Jeffrey R. Holland succinctly summarized the events that had transpired thus far: "The cultural freedom of the Renaissance and religious freedom of the Reformation underscored the strong sense of personal freedom espoused in the Enlightenment to provide the ideal attitudes and environments for the beginning of [America]" ("A Promised Land," *Ensign,* June 1976, 23).

Following the discovery of America, Europeans sought new opportunity and religious freedom on its shores. Most notable among them were the Puritans, who left England to establish a religious covenant with God away from the persecutions and conditions of their mother country. The Puritans were especially aware of the importance of America in the Lord's work, and Jonathan Edwards—perhaps the greatest intellectual among them—made a stunningly accurate prediction during the first Great Awakening (mid-1700s) about what would soon unfold in America:

> This new world is probably now discovered, that the new and most glorious state of God's church on earth might commence there; that God might in it begin a new world in a spiritual respect. . . .
>
> And it is worthy to be noted, that America was discovered about the time of the reformation, or but little before: which reformation was the first thing that God did towards the glorious renovation of the world, after it had sunk into the depths of darkness and ruin, under the great anti-Christian apostasy. . . .
>
> And if we may suppose that this glorious work of God shall begin in any part of America, I think, if we consider the circumstances of the settlement of New England, it must needs appear the most likely, of all American colonies, to be the place whence this work shall principally take its rise. And, if these things be so, it gives

us more abundant reason to hope that what is now seen in America, and especially in New England, may prove the dawn of that glorious day; and the very uncommon and wonderful circumstances and events of this work, seem to me strongly to argue that God intends it as the beginning or forerunner of something vastly great. ("The Latter-day Glory Is Probably to Begin in America").

Soon after this Great Awakening, America won its independence from Great Britain and in time established the U.S. Constitution, which provided for political and religious liberty. America did not accomplish this alone, however, for the hand of Providence had been manifested many times in its behalf. James Madison, one of many of the Founders who testified of this miraculous power, wrote, "It is impossible for the man of pious reflection not to perceive in it [the Constitution], a finger of that Almighty hand which has been so frequently and so signally extended to our relief in the critical stages of the revolution" ("Federalist Papers," essay 37).

President Ezra Taft Benson had this to say about the Constitution:

> Every Latter-day Saint should love the inspired Constitution of the United States—a nation with a spiritual foundation and a prophetic history—which nation the Lord has declared to be his base of operations in these latter days.
>
> The framers of the Constitution were men raised up by God to establish this foundation of our government, for so the Lord has decreed by revelation in these words:
>
> "I established the Constitution of this land, by the hands of *wise men whom I raised up unto this very purpose,* and redeemed the land by the shedding of blood (D&C 101:80; italics added)" ("The Constitution—A Glorious Standard," *Ensign,* May 1976, 91).

The Lord said that our divine Constitution "belongs to *all* mankind . . ." and that it "should be maintained for the rights and protection of *all* flesh, according to just and holy principles" (D&C 98:5; 101:77; italics added). "The Constitution of the United States has served as a model for many nations," wrote President Benson, "and is the oldest constitution in use today. . . . For centuries the Lord kept America hidden in the hollow of His hand until the time was right to unveil her for her destiny in the last days. . . . Our Father in heaven planned the coming forth of the Founding Fathers and their form of government as the necessary great prologue leading to the restoration of the gospel" ("Our Divine Constitution, *Ensign,* November 1987, 4–5).

Similarly, President Wilford Woodruff declared, "Those men who laid the foundation of this American government were the best spirits the God of heaven could find on the face of the earth. They were choice spirits . . . [and] were inspired of the Lord" (Conference Report, April 1898, 89).

Preparation of the Prophet

Now that we have seen the Lord's hand in establishing the general conditions for the Restoration, let us turn to Joseph Smith's lineage and the timing of his placement in upstate New York. Joseph Smith was preordained, much like Moses, Job, and other biblical prophets, to a special mission, and his name was known by prophets thousands of years before his birth. Joseph of Egypt prophesied, "Thus saith the Lord unto me: A choice seer will I raise up out of the fruit of thy loins. . . . And his name shall be called after me; and it shall be after the name of his father. And he shall be like unto me; for the thing, which the Lord shall bring forth by his hand, by the power of the Lord shall bring my people unto salvation" (2 Nephi 3:7, 15). It is interesting that Joseph Smith Sr. named his third son, not his first, Joseph.

Beyond Joseph's Israelite lineage, both of his immediate parents were deeply religious, having experienced divine manifestations, including heavenly dreams and heavenly voices. At the time when Joseph was a boy, one last condition presented itself that stirred him to search for truth. The second Great Awakening caught hold in his community and produced a spirit of revivalism for the Christian faith. Various sects proselytized heavily for new converts, and Joseph wrote, "After our removal to Manchester, there was in the place where we lived an unusual excitement on the subject of religion. . . . Indeed, the whole district of country seemed affected by it, and great multitudes united themselves to the different religious parties, which created no small stir and division amongst the people, some crying, 'Lo, here!' and others, 'Lo, there!'" (Joseph Smith—History 1:5).

In turn, Joseph intensely reflected and studied religion and soon decided to take the subject to the Lord. Therefore, when Joseph Smith entered the Sacred Grove, all eyes of heaven were upon him. All those who had gone before him to prepare the way were watching; all those who would come after him were hoping. The Lord spent centuries preparing for this moment, providing a lineage that traced its roots back to Abraham. Indeed, Joseph's prayer was not only his own but also the prayer of all mankind. And in response to that prayer, God the Eternal Father and his beloved Son appeared to young Joseph Smith and began the process of restoring light and truth to the world.

The Significance of the First Vision

Consider the meaning of this magnificent theophany. When the vision closed and Joseph was left to himself, he walked back to his family's farmhouse and resumed his everyday life. Outwardly he appeared to be the same person. But what had happened?

Through this glorious experience in the Sacred Grove, a profound change had begun to take place in Joseph's mind and heart. Unlike the rest of mankind, he now had a correct idea of God. He had seen that the Father and the Son were actual persons. And as they called him by name and spoke to him, he must have felt that he was of great worth. The Savior not only answered his question but also told him "many other things" (Joseph Smith—History 1:18–20). Eventually he came to know that God was literally *his* Father and that Jesus Christ was *his* elder brother, and he came to understand how precious and important *he* was.

Why did the Lord *begin* the events of the Restoration with a personal appearance to the young Joseph Smith? Why would this kind of attention and this information be given him at the very outset? The First Vision is important for many reasons, but I believe its greatest significance is that it reveals our true identity and our relationship with God. What Joseph Smith got was an accurate map or paradigm, not only about who God is but also about who he was and who we are. A knowledge of these truths is essential to our eternal progress, and it can come to each of us only in the way it came to Joseph Smith—by divine revelation, or through parents or teachers who transmit the truths given originally by revelation. The reason that is so is because only God knows fully our true identity.

Social and Divine Self-Concepts

Without revelation, our perceptions of God and of ourselves come from the *social mirror*—the reflection of all those things that have been programmed into our mental and emotional software by our upbringing and our culture. No matter how great the capacity of a computer's hardware, only the software, the programming, can release that potential. Thus the output of the computer is strictly limited by the capacity of the software.

It is the same with human beings. Every person on earth is *literally* God's son or daughter and therefore has infinite potential. But if we believe that we are merely God's *creatures,* fundamentally and unalterably different in nature and inferior to him, our sense of self-worth and our capacity to reach our divine potential will be severely restricted. We are literally his children, spiritually begotten. In our "spirit DNA" we are one generation from Elohim, our Eternal Father.

We cannot act outside our perception of who we are. Our potential is utterly limited by it, although in fact our potential is unlimited. If we see ourselves as failures, if we have had that drummed into our minds and hearts our whole lives long, it is difficult to rise above that programming. On the other hand, if we really understand something of our true potential, our divine heritage, we become uncomfortable being anything less than what we know we should be.

One woman who has worked with troubled youth as a foster mother has experienced firsthand the kind of changes that can occur when people learn who they really are. She writes:

> The children who come into my home usually have extremely low self-esteem, and their behaviors are quite often magnified because they have no sense of worth. I have focused on trying to help build up their self-esteem by giving them a sense that they are children of our Heavenly Father, that they are of worth, that my time is important and I choose to spend it with them because they are so important. As I start to teach these kids and

reinforce in them that they are children of God, I have seen some pretty remarkable changes occur.

There is one boy in particular who has had a mighty change since he has developed more of an understanding of his divine identity. When he came into my home, he was a thirteen-year-old with a serious attitude problem. He had come from a single-parent home that was not secure. His mother would leave him with relatives or friends at every chance, dropping him off for sometimes even a year or two, until his attitude and behavior became so disruptive that nobody would keep him anymore.

He grew to be angry and mean, and his only desire in life was to be a gangster, so he dressed and acted like one. He wore his big baggy pants and earrings, and he resisted everything and did whatever he could to upset me. I listened and prayed and did everything I could to help him understand that he was a child of God. He began to see that I could have respect for him as a child of our Heavenly Father, even though he had these negative behaviors. He learned that I expected more out of him than that, and his behavior did change.

He's been steady with me for four years now and has thrived in the security of the knowledge that Heavenly Father gives his life value and that I care about him. He wears very nice clothes now and cares about his appearance. His personality has changed. In fact, one time some kids were teasing my daughter, and she was feeling bad about it, and when I walked into the room, this boy had tears in his eyes. I see him mirroring the fact that not only is he of worth, but others are as well.

In the mission field, we wrote to every person who joined the Church in our mission to learn what they thought were the key elements in their conversion. One theme recurred over and over in all of those letters. It was this: They never really doubted the Church and the gospel, but they often doubted themselves. They doubted their worthiness, their basic capacity to live up to what was going to be expected of them. They were overlaid with a kind of cultural software that defined them as not being "spiritual."

If the only images we ever saw of ourselves were the caricatures in carnival fun-house mirrors, they would become our reality, and we would think, "This is what I am. This is what I look like." In the same way, if our upbringing gives us a false definition of ourselves, and if that definition is continually reinforced by our experiences with family members, teachers, peers, and others, the evidence accumulates until we thoroughly believe it, saying to ourselves, "This is who I am." So the key in those people's conversion became the testimony and affirmation of the missionaries of their true, divine nature, of their divine potential and capacity to receive Christ and his gospel and truly become part of his work and kingdom. The truth of these ideas penetrated their hearts through the influence of the Holy Spirit.

What happens when those with a false self-concept are consistently told they are children of God? They may consider it an interesting idea, but they may only intellectualize it at first. They may even be unable to internalize it, because their false self-concept is so deeply embedded in their minds and hearts that they don't even question it. Again, a full awareness of our true identity can come only by revelation. One young convert to the Church tells how she received this witness:

> I was nineteen when I was introduced to the gospel
> of Jesus Christ. Prior to gaining a knowledge that I was a
> spirit daughter of God and that my life did in fact have
> meaning, purpose, and direction, my heart was a bundle

of worries and confusions. Although I felt some sort of affinity toward God, I did not understand what my *relationship* was with him, and therefore, I could not *relate to* him. Without being able to really relate to him, I had no way of understanding how the pieces of my life were any more significant than the pieces of a cardboard puzzle.

When I was taught the gospel by missionaries, I was forced to confront the Lord through prayer. These missionaries exhorted me time and time again to pray. They asked me what my feelings were when I prayed. I was sort of uncomfortable praying at first, but they wouldn't let me off the hook. They revisited the question of prayer in each discussion. At first, I would just answer that I felt "good." As I continued to apply the principles they were teaching me in my life and to pray about them, though, I felt more than good. I felt joy. I was, for the first time in my life, developing and understanding this relationship I had with my Father in Heaven. I was realizing that my life was not a random series of experiences but rather a continuation of experiences in a greater scheme of life and eternity than I had ever known. I learned that because of this "greater scheme," I could return to live with my Father in Heaven if I chose to follow the Lord through the course of my life.

We Are of the Father

I once spoke on the subject of the divine self-definition at the Missionary Training Center in Provo, Utah. Afterward a missionary came up to me and asked, "Would you look me in the eye and say those things again?"

I turned to him and said, "You are God's child. He loves you perfectly. You have infinite worth, infinite potential, and you are not to be compared."

Tears started streaming down his cheeks. "Brother Covey, would you please say those words to me just once more?"

I looked at him intently and told him, "You are God's own child. He loves you with an infinite love. You have infinite potential and worth. You are not to compare yourself with anyone else, because God doesn't."

This missionary was basically saying that he had never *heard* these things before, but he heard them that day because the Holy Spirit communicated them to his mind and heart. He had probably heard them many times, but he had not yet had the experience of *spiritually* hearing them, of feeling them deeply and internalizing them. He was beginning to get into the spirit of his mission, and the Lord was teaching him—through the scriptures, through the prophets, through his teachers, and especially through the Holy Ghost—what his true identity was.

As I said earlier, I believe that the true significance of the First Vision is that it tells us who God really is and who we really are. Joseph Smith once said, "If men do not comprehend the character of God, they do not comprehend themselves" (*Teachings of the Prophet Joseph Smith,* 343). Brigham Young added a corollary to that principle: "No man can know himself unless he knows God, and he cannot know God unless he knows himself" (*Discourses of Brigham Young,* 426). In other words, knowledge of ourselves and knowledge of God are completely interrelated, because we are of the same lineage.

Sheri Dew, former counselor in the general Relief Society presidency, testified, "That we are here now is no accident. For aeons of time our Father watched us and knew He could trust us when so much would be at stake. We have been held in reserve for this very hour. We need to understand not just who we are but who we have always been" ("Stand Tall and Stand Together," *Ensign,* November 2000, 94).

I had the opportunity to share these principles with several of the counselors in the Especially for Youth program administered by the Church Educational System, and they had some remarkable experiences with the youth who came through the program that summer. One counselor told of a group of four tough boys who did not want to be there and didn't want to participate in any of the activities. One afternoon they sneaked back to their dorm room and tried to brand each other with a key heated up by a cigarette lighter. Having broken one of the major rules, they might have been sent home, but the counselor felt that they needed to stay, so she sat them down to try to work through this problem. In her words:

> We started to talk about *why* it was important for them to respect their bodies—it was because they were children of Heavenly Father. He had created them. And as we sat and talked about that, I saw a light turn on. They began to understand who they really were, and the walls began to come down. We talked about the peer pressure that had caused them to brand each other, and all of a sudden one of the young men clued in and started talking to the other three. He said, "Do you guys understand that this is a problem, and this is why it's wrong?" They finally figured out why they were in trouble and why we were concerned about them.
>
> I let them stay, and we became really good friends. It was amazing to see that once they finally understood who they were, everything else fell into place for them that week. They started learning during the classes, and at night they would stay up late and read their scriptures

together. When they understood who they were, and they understood their relationship with Heavenly Father, they were finally able to get down on their knees and pray for answers for other questions and concerns they were struggling with. They had come to EFY with the goal of ruining all the activities, and by the end of the week they were talking about how to help one another get on missions.

I feel especially fortunate and blessed to have had parents and grandparents who have communicated and affirmed my worth and potential and innate divine nature from my childhood up. My mother's father was Stephen L Richards, who was an apostle and later the first counselor to President David O. McKay. He was constantly affirming his posterity's true nature. In a general conference address, he expressed it this way:

> The eternal spirit of man became housed in a tabernacle of flesh in the likeness of the Father, and the sons of God began life upon the earth. They were not menial nor of low or servile nature. They were of high estate, of the noblest lineage, endowed with the God-given gift of intelligence or the light of truth, the sublime and supreme investiture of both God and man, the eternal verity which 'was not created or made, neither indeed can be.' This *intelligence* not only gave man superiority over all other creations but, even more importantly, it brought him *consciousness* of his relationship to God and the world and envisaged for him the purpose and destiny of his life (Conference Report, April 1939, 38; emphasis added).

Scarcity versus Abundance

These truths have a profound impact on the way we feel toward ourselves and other people. President Brigham Young explained, "When we know ourselves, we know our neighbors. When we know precisely how to deal with ourselves, we know how to deal with our neighbors" (*Discourses of Brigham Young,* 269).

But if we do not have a deep sense of our true identity, if our basic sense of self comes from other people, we may develop a view of life based on scarcity rather than charity or abundance. A *scarcity mentality* is the tendency to define oneself in terms of being better than, or not as good as, another person. It involves the idea that there is only so much to go around, as if there were only one pie out there, and if someone gets a big piece of the pie, that means there is less for everyone else.

People with a scarcity mentality have a difficult time being genuinely happy for the successes of others, even family members or close friends. When they see another person receive special recognition or good fortune, it's almost as if something is being taken away from them. They might verbally express happiness for the other person's success, but inwardly they are eating their hearts out, and they know it. Sometimes they even harbor a secret delight in hearing about the misfortunes or weaknesses of others, especially those whom others may have regarded as heroes. They're always competing, always comparing.

I know of one young woman who struggled head-on with the "cancer" of comparing. She found herself on the short end of the social stick, heartbroken about the comparisons and possible rejection. I remember saying to her how much God loved her for her own sake and that she should not compare herself to anybody else, that if she could become increasingly Christ-centered, the tendency to compare would recede and might eventually be eliminated altogether. She wouldn't feel the pain of people's anticipated judgments of her because she would feel so strongly the love of the Lord.

She could hardly believe me at first. Her school culture had so ingrained in her that she needed to have all the right clothes, all the right friends, all the right mannerisms, even down to a certain kind of hairstyle. She was so deeply engaged in the system of basing her self-worth on comparison with others that she simply could not see another way of determining her worth.

People with a scarcity mind-set like that young woman had actually like hearing about the weaknesses of others. It makes them feel justified and at least equal. Just look at the obsession some people have gossiping about other people's weaknesses. It's just a clear case of a lack of charity. As one wise soul said, "When man found the mirror, he began to lose his soul." The point is, he became more concerned with his image than with his self.

The apostle Paul said that "charity envieth not; . . . seeketh not her own, . . . thinketh no evil; rejoiceth not in iniquity" (1 Corinthians 13:4–6). Charity, or the pure love of Christ, produces an abundance mentality so that we're never threatened by the successes of other people. We don't get hung up on position or credentials, associations or affiliations, good looks or fashion. As we are introduced into a celestial culture, the culture of the external world becomes relatively unimportant to us.

Where do we get the scarcity mentality? Is it just our nature? I suggest it is not; it is a *learned* nature. The notion of scarcity comes out of social conditioning—being compared with siblings, being graded on a curve, participating in school athletics or popularity contests, and so forth. Athletic experiences in particular continually pump competitive blood through the bodies, hearts, and minds of participants. Some children raised in family climates of abundance learn the scarcity mentality through highly competitive high school athletics. Here children are often taught that winning is the main end, rather than skill development, growth, and fun. Interestingly, truly great coaches and teams tend to view competition more as a measuring stick of their own personal development. When asked about how he scouted other teams, John Wooden, who earned more NCAA basketball titles than any other coach, replied, "We only worry about doing our best." In his paradigm of competition, it is possible to lose and still have a successful game.

For those with a scarcity mentality, a comparison-based identity, the big issue of life becomes fairness, and often the dominant goal is to win, to beat others, to be number one. But the whole scarcity concept is a flawed, apostate notion. It creates an unhealthy hunger to get ahead, to have more, to be more, and it leads to all kinds of prejudices, judgments, and labels. In the words of C. S. Lewis, "Pride gets no pleasure out of having something, only out of having more of it than the next man" (*Mere Christianity,* 109). It's hard to love other people completely with a scarcity mind-set. It's hard to experience charity, which is "the pure love of Christ" (Moroni 7:47).

Ironically, however, the pure love of Christ is the only real antidote to a scarcity mentality, because people must truly *feel* this love before they can get a sense of self from the divine source. Jesus said, "I am come that they might have life, and that they might have it more abundantly" (John 10:10). In other words, he taught us an *abundance mentality.* This Christ-centered mind-set flows from the knowledge of who we really are and from the deep inner sense of personal worth and security that accompanies that knowledge. It assures us that we have no need to make comparisons or compete with others, because the love of our Heavenly Father and our Savior is unlimited. Having an abundance mentality enables us to live with joy and cheerfulness; it enables us to have faith and hope and the other positive ideas that come with a correct paradigm that says the Lord is in charge here, and that he knows us for who we really, divinely are.

One woman who had gone through a divorce found her self-concept floundering until she discovered these truths:

> Although I feel like I have been through a lot of trials in my life, there has been nothing like going through a divorce. At first, I couldn't believe this was happening to me and my family. When we were sealed in the temple, I truly believed that it was forever. I think what I struggled with the most was the emotional implications of being divorced. I really struggled with an overwhelming sense of failure. I felt like I was such a failure—that I had failed myself, my children, and Heavenly Father. During the darkest of days there was one thing that I continued to hold on to, and that was the knowledge that I am a child of God. That belief grounded me and got me through a lot of difficulty. I spent a lot of time on my knees, and he told me that I was his and that he loved me.

When people understand their relationship with God, the transformation in their lives reflects the abundance mentality, as in the case of the following sister, related by a missionary in her area:

> A few months after arriving in this city we were tracting, and the man who opened one door said, "Oh, yeah, I know who you are." We immediately thought, *He's going to think we're Jehovah's Witnesses,* because that's what everybody always thought we were. He said, "You're the Mormon elders, aren't you? My sister belongs to your church."
>
> When we told him that we knew her, he said, "I only have one question for you. I really don't have any interest in joining your church, but I want to know something. What have you done to her?" Of course, we had

no idea what he was talking about. He said, "Well, you didn't know her before she joined your church." And he told us the story right there at his doorstep—the story of a woman who had no interest in raising a family, who thought that it was her duty to raise the kids, but did not want to be involved in their lives. She was a chain-smoker and had absolutely no concept of who she was, not even a value system of taking care of herself. Her hair was unkempt, and she would go to the store in her sweats or her nightgown. She did not care about herself or her home.

I could not believe this, because the sister I knew was a beautiful woman. Her hair was always in place, and she was dressed immaculately when she came to church. She didn't have the money to buy expensive clothes, but she cared for the ones that she did have. When we went to her home, it was spotless. So with that background, I approached her, and I said, "You know, we ran into your brother."

She said, "Oh, what did he tell you?"

I said, "Well, let's just say there's been a magnificent transformation," and I asked her to tell me about it.

She told me, "It's when I found out who I was. I'm a child of God. Why shouldn't I be a queen on this earth? I have to live up to this reputation." A light had turned on for her, and even her living environment changed. She decided that she wanted her home to be an abode where a child of God would live.

When she understood who she was, she knew that her children were also children of God. They were married by that time, but she wanted to be involved in their lives. She wanted to influence them as a giver of light. Her attitude changed from "What's in it for me?" to "I'm here for you."

In working with the scarcity/abundance continuum over the years, I've learned that just having an awareness of it is like being halfway toward overcoming the scarcity mentality. The other half is achieved through applying the power of the gospel and practicing abundance thinking and skills. But it's been amazing to see the almost-immediate impact of simply becoming self-aware of the almost universal, deep-seated tendency toward scarcity thinking, and the almost universal, deep-seated capacity for abundance thinking. It's almost as if we have assumed that scarcity and comparison-based thinking are "just the way things are." But the moment we make that assumption explicit and challenge it by looking through a gospel lens, we are introduced into a new, exciting, expanding worldview.

Reflecting the Divine Mirror

Again, you and I are God's own children. We have infinite potential, infinite worth, and we should not compare ourselves with others in any way on the basis of status, position, appearance, fashion, or any of the world's value systems. All of these systems are false sources of self-definition, and we are surrounded by them. We live in a media-saturated world that continuously tries to define who we are. Unless we counteract these false scripts, they become deeply planted in our hearts and minds and also in the hearts and minds of our children.

When I was teaching at Brigham Young University, I frequently asked my students to test their self-perception. On the left side of a paper they wrote down how others perceived them, starting with their families and working down through friends, teachers, and so on. On the right side of the page, they wrote down how God saw them, based on what the scriptures, the prophets, the Atonement, and their patriarchal blessings said. At the bottom of the page, they were to answer the question "How do you perceive yourself?" Invariably, two-thirds of the students saw themselves based on the social, not the divine mirror.

One way we can counteract this kind of social conditioning is to reflect *to each other* the divine mirror that was given to Joseph Smith in the Sacred Grove. That is, in addition to bearing testimony of God, Christ, the prophets, and the Restoration, we can bear testimony of *people* and who they really are. We can look into the eyes of our children or others and say, "You are God's own child. You are of infinite worth, and you have divine potential."

The Psalmist once asked God why he was concerned with us mortals at all: "What is man, that thou art mindful of him? and the son of man, that thou visitest him?" Then he gave the answer: "Thou hast made him a little lower than the angels, and hast crowned him with glory and honour" (Psalm 8:4–5). As mortals, we are just a little lower than the angels, but in fact we and the angels potentially have a divine state.

Joseph Smith taught that people must first rely on "human testimony" for their knowledge of God before they can obtain a divine testimony of his character, perfections, and attributes (see *Lectures on Faith,* 2:33, 55–56, Questions and Answers). If our first contacts with human beings are not affirming and positive, will we not look on the divine through the lens of those negative experiences? Missionaries are taught this daily through their experiences. They must first show unconditional caring and love before people will be open to and trust their testimony and teaching. To bring people to the Savior of the world, the missionaries must be like him, particularly "when push comes to shove"—

when they are rejected and reviled against. Many people have had traumatic human experiences that cause them to mistrust all expressions of sincere caring and love unless those expressions are tested to the point of sacrifice. We often talk about becoming saviors on Mount Zion for those who are dead, but we can also work to bring about the salvation of the living.

Affirming Others

One of the most important things we can do as parents, teachers, and leaders is to *affirm* people—to believe in them, see their innate potential, and treat them accordingly, to elevate them in their own eyes. Not only should we testify of their true identity, but in many cases we should ignore their inappropriate behavior and simply reassure them of their infinite capacity and potential. One high school teacher writes of the power of this principle:

> I was a first-year teacher at a new school in a rough area. It wasn't the high school experience I was used to. My first few weeks consisted of breaking up gang fights, being cursed and yelled at and physically threatened, having my personal property stolen, scrubbing graffiti off the walls and desks of my classroom, trying to control an uncontrollable situation. When the bell finally rang on a Friday afternoon at the end of a very long week, all I could think of was getting home and away from these kids. I had packed up my stuff and was ready to leave when I noticed that my keys were missing. I searched and searched until a student finally told me that one of the other students in my class had stolen my keys. I ran to see if my car was still in the parking lot, and upon finding it gone I sat down in the parking lot and cried. This was the final straw; I had had it.

That night I told my husband I was quitting on Monday. No job was worth this. He said he would support me in whatever I chose to do but suggested that I really pray about it before I made a final decision. All weekend long I prayed, hoping that Heavenly Father would agree with my decision.

Monday morning came, and I still hadn't felt like I had received a confirmation of my decision, so I went to school filled with dread. As I sat in my first class with kids screaming and yelling, I pleaded silently with my Heavenly Father that if he wanted me to stay, he would show me why. I looked out upon the chaos, and all I saw was a few individual faces. It was as if I was viewing them with someone else's eyes, and I was filled with love for them. I felt so deeply the love Heavenly Father had for them, and I knew why I was there and why I needed to stay. I felt the Spirit tell me that they were his children, and I was there to show them that he loved them when they thought they were all alone.

From that day on everything changed. Well, *I* did. I saw each student as a son or daughter of God, and I honestly tried to teach them accordingly. I began to listen to them, ask them questions, take an interest in their lives, and attend their activities. Nothing changed at first—they still threatened me and yelled at me. But gradually, as they kept pushing me away and I still came back with love and support, some of them began to open up. They actually began to listen when I taught, and to my amazement they participated and did their work.

I became pregnant with my first child during that school year, and these kids whom so many called "hopeless" began to serve me. Some would carry my books, while others brought me soup and crackers to try to settle my stomach. One of my toughest students, a gang member who had been in and out of youth detention centers, brought me a teddy bear to give to my baby when it was born. He told me how lucky my child was to have me as a mother. He said if he could have felt that love every day of his life, he could have been a different person. I told him how wonderful he was, and that he could be the person he wanted to be. He said he was just starting to realize that.

After that first year I stopped teaching to stay home with my daughter. The teddy bear is on a shelf in her room to serve as a reminder of the power of love. Every day I pray for the gift to see her through the eyes He once allowed me to see through in a small, stuffy classroom in the "ghetto."

The Affirming Power of Love

When I was a mission president, one of the missionaries wasn't having the success he wanted to have, and he didn't know what to do. In our monthly interview, he said, "If I went home it would just about kill my parents. Could you assign me to a building mission so I can build buildings? I love to build—I know about that." I began listening deeply, empathetically, to him, because I realized he had never experienced the first event with anybody—not with me, not with his companions. Then he started to open up, and he told me about the promises he had been given of all the baptisms he would have in the mission field. He said, "I've worked my heart out, but I've had none of these promises fulfilled." I said to myself, *We've got to get some unconditional love into this elder, because until he learns to love unconditionally, these blessings will not come to pass.* He thought they would come simply through hard work, but that was not the case.

So I found him a companion who knew how to be empathetic. He was a leader. And I said, "I'm asking you to take this elder for at least two or three months. I'm sorry you're not going to be a zone leader anymore, but this is just that important." He was totally willing to do it. He loved that elder as no one had ever loved him before. He listened to him. He never judged him or compared him with others. Instead, he modeled how to love people and how to listen within their frame of reference. Then this elder began to think, "Oh, this is how you do it." And he gradually learned how.

After about three months I said to him, "Will you stay just during this next companionship? Then if you still want to go on a building mission, we'll work that out." He said he would stay *for good,* because now he understood his true identity and how to affirm the true identity of others. It was the first time anyone had ever got him into the gospel—*really* into the gospel. He had merely been active in the Church; to tap into this other energy, this true source of love, was the key.

I believe if we will learn to love people, it will optimize their growth. It won't guarantee it, because all people have their agency. But it increases the likelihood of their development. Listen to what people are saying with their hearts. Receive them to yourself. Don't be so quick to rush in with your teachings. You really can't influence people until they feel they have influence with you. Most people don't listen with the intent to understand; they listen with the intent to reply. So listen with the intent to understand. Once you understand, then you can teach, because you have received the person yourself, and now you can share of your-self with the person.

We have to begin on the level of the person we are trying to help. I have dear friends who are serving a part-time inner-city mission as their Church calling. They tell me that they focus almost entirely on meeting the most pressing and obvious needs of the people in their area, such as finding a job, making ends meet, dealing with major discipline problems in the family, try-ing to get custody after a divorce proceeding, getting the home and family clean and organized, and dealing with different kinds of health problems, sanitary issues, abuse, violence, and on and on. I asked my friends if they try to teach the gospel. They basi-cally said, "No. All we are doing is just meeting the urgent needs of the moment, of survival, and coping with life itself."

That reminds me of the Savior spending a good portion of his time doing exactly this kind of work: healing, feeding, meet-ing basic needs before he attempted to teach the truths of the kingdom. Relationships must be established first—caring, affirm-ing, serving relationships.

On my first mission in Great Britain, I was close to a very powerful and persuasive elder who was instrumental in converting an extremely competent and successful businessman. This con-vert was ultimately called by the Brethren to be a stake president. The elder who had converted him, on returning home from his mission, fell into an intellectual state of apostasy, and after obtain-ing several advanced degrees, became a prominent academician. His was the classic case warned of by Jacob in the Book of Mormon: "When they are learned they think they are wise, and they hearken not unto the counsel of God, for they set it aside, supposing they know of themselves" (2 Nephi 9:28).

At that time, stake presidents were invited annually to attend general conference, probably so they could get a vision of the larger Church and receive instruction and training. The stake president had heard how his converting elder had fallen away, and he wanted to see him on one of these trips to general conference. They communicated with each other and made arrangements to meet in New York when the president changed planes there on his way back to England after the conference had concluded. They were to have spent at least two hours with each other, but because of mechanical problems on the flight from Salt Lake City to New York, they ended up having only two minutes.

If you were this stake president, what would you do if you could spend just two minutes face-to-face with the missionary who had brought you into the Church and who himself had fallen away? Just think about what words you would say, what you would do. You have only two minutes as you run from one gate to catch your international flight at another gate.

This humble, faithful stake president was very wise. What he said and did demonstrated the power and importance of affirming another person. He said to the elder, "Elder, it's marvelous to see you. I am so happy to see you. You taught me the gospel and brought me into the Church, and have blessed my life and the life of my family eternally. I cannot thank you enough."

Then, having given this powerful affirmation to the disaffected elder, the president asked one simple question that stirred the young man into temporary humility and a sense of stewardship again: "I have given my whole life to this Church—have I made a mistake?"

There was a long pause, and the stake president let the Spirit do its work in that pause. In other words, he submitted himself again to this elder, his teacher. The elder started to tear up, and then he broke down and said, "No, you have not made a mistake, but I have." They embraced, and the stake president ran to his next flight.

The key to human influence is first to be influenced—that is, to first understand where people's hearts and heads are. When the stake president showed his willingness to be influenced by the elder, he brought the barriers down.

My son David learned this principle himself when he was on his mission. One particular contact had no interest at all in David's message, but when David saw this man's interest in the Beatles and expressed his own liking for their music, a connection was formed and a relationship established. The trust and identification in that relationship opened up a communication channel so the gospel could be taught and received. A few years later, the man was ordained a bishop.

Affirming Our Families

Having a true sense of our identity gives us security and overcomes our tendency to judge. Parents should rear their children in this concept; we should affirm others in it. As a parent, one of the most important things you can do is to never disbelieve in your kids. Just keep believing in them, seeing in them the celestial spirit that is there, even in wayward children like those with a drug problem. You *don't* look at their behavior. You look at their divine identity and potential and treat them accordingly. How do you do that? Well, if you don't have deep within yourself this same sense, you can't. You may try to fake it, but it won't come genuinely, authentically, except from the soul of those who sense it about themselves and their relationship to God, who gives us the eye of faith.

If you have teenagers, smile a lot. Don't take their insensitivity personally. Roll with the punches and remember that "this too shall pass." Don't get angry and empower their weaknesses as they go through their identity crises. Stay true and faithful to them. Hold them accountable through a system of discipline, not punishment, and give them your constant love.

Remember that someday there might be a life-changing event that will shift a wayward teen's paradigm, as one young man experienced:

> I had been inactive for a number of years and I saw no need for the Church or for a God in my life. I had a hard time understanding how there could be a God, let alone a loving God, with all the horrific things that took place in the world. I especially didn't believe that a God, if there was one, knew me and cared about what happened in my life. So I stopped going to church and began to live the type of life I thought I always wanted.
>
> I married, and after a few years my wife became pregnant. At the time, my wife and I didn't have a very strong relationship, and I found myself spending as much time as possible away from home. I grew tired of the constant fighting, and the pressure I felt every time I looked at her and knew that she was having my child. I wasn't ready to be a father and did not want the responsibility that came with that new role.
>
> But something happened when my first child was born. When I held that little child in my arms, I knew. I looked into my son's eyes and saw the love my Heavenly Father had for me, and at that moment I knew that I was a son of God and that my new little son was a son of God. This moment changed my life. It was as if the plan seemed to unfold. There wasn't anything I wouldn't do

for this little being, and I knew that must be how Heavenly Father felt about me.

I felt I was loved in that small hospital birthing room, and that love carried me through the road of repentance. When I felt the love and forgiveness come into my life, I became a new man. I became a husband and developed a relationship with my wife and my son. We stopped arguing as much, and I found myself longing to be at home when I was away. I hadn't felt that desire in a very long time. Knowing who I was changed how I treated my wife and how I viewed my role as a father. I wanted to be a father, and the joy of being with my son filled my life.

When we affirm our family members and others as children of God, we're helping them *experience* the first event of the Restoration on a personal level. We're helping them understand that they have the potential of godhood built into them. Our objective is not to set ourselves up as models but rather to help them discover that Christ is the model—the perfect model that can eclipse and subordinate the false and restrictive models of the world.

While recently providing professional leadership training in South Africa to many people who were working with victims of AIDS and the HIV virus, I met one of the most powerful, saintly, and beautiful women it has been my privilege to know. They called her "Mamma Jackie." She worked extensively with the orphans of those who died from the AIDS infection and with many of the troubled teenage youth. I asked her what was the most important lesson she had learned in working with these people. Her answer was simple and profound: "People feel important when *they* are important to other people. So this is what I do.

I involve young people to identify those who are worse off than *they* are and then to serve them."

Service, of course, is the essence of what the Savior and his restored Church teach. That is the model Christ gave us. It is noteworthy that one of the greatest ways for people to have a sense of their own worth and potential, their own identity, comes from their becoming important to other people in meeting their needs and in serving their temporal and spiritual welfare. What a contrast this is from the popular psychology, that the best way to build self-esteem is to get people to think positively about themselves!

Internalizing the First Event

The basic, personal initiative I suggest taking with regard to the first event is to offer daily, listening prayers of faith. The key to prayer, I have found, is listening, just as the Prophet Joseph listened to the Father introduce the Son, who answered his question.

Consider all the preparation the Lord inspired in creating the necessary conditions for Joseph's prayers and the Lord's answer. These same preparations can apply to our own understanding of prayer. Let's start with the Apostasy. At a personal level, we may be keenly aware of some of our own sins, either of commission—wrongdoing—or of omission—simply not doing good or being casual about sacred responsibilities. This may lead us to a desire to repent. Otherwise, using Brigham Young's words, we may "pray against counsel."

The Renaissance would be analogous to opening our minds and our hearts for the need to learn, to grow, to continue this repentance, and "to look out." The Reformation would be analogous to repenting of that which we know we need to repent of, and to open the scriptures, and to "look in" as well as "look up."

The Enlightenment and the first Great Awakening would be

analogous to listening to our consciences and combining reason and faith. The discovery and colonization of the New World would be analogous to changing our environment so that we are surrounded by uplifting circumstances, inspiring teachers and leaders, and supportive loved ones. The establishment of the divinely inspired Constitution would be analogous to building some orderly structures and positive habits into our lives.

The second Great Awakening of Joseph's day may be analogous to making up our minds to also believe James when he taught us to ask of God, and that "if he gave wisdom to them that lacked wisdom, and would give liberally, and not upbraid, I might venture" (Joseph Smith—History 1:13). This might lead us to our own Sacred Grove that we would never wish to leave in our hearts and in our minds.

The Lord said of the religionists of Joseph's day, "They draw near to me with their lips, but their hearts are far from me" (Joseph Smith—History 1:19). The ear of the spirit, I suggest, is the heart. That's where the listening takes place. This kind of listening requires earnest, sincere openness. A genuinely two-way communication makes us a little vulnerable, because we don't know what's going to happen.

Sometimes we pray as if we had a checklist in hand. We give instructions or make requests of the Lord to our bidding as if he were some kind of cosmic servant. This type of prayer is often vain, empty, centered on personal wants, with little connection to the heart—the ear of the spirit. The key to real, effective praying is to exercise faith in our prayers, knowing that we are speaking to a living, loving God in the name of his beloved Son, and that he wants to bless us in his way and according to his will.

In the mission field, we encouraged our missionaries to keep "faith journals." They began each morning with a prayer of faith, first asking to know what the will of the Father was for them on that particular day. Then they would spend time listening to know what commitments they needed to make and keep in order to gain the blessings and wisdom they sought. Finally, in the journal, they would write down the blessings they had prayed for and the commitments they had made to obey the laws upon which those blessings were predicated. At the end of the day, they would take out the faith journal, examine their level of keeping their commitments, and record the results. Gradually, their faith in the power of their prayers became stronger and stronger. You might consider if such an approach would also work for you.

The more we listen in our prayers, the more we will begin to think in terms of our *needs* rather than our *wants*—particularly our needs as the Lord would perceive them. It's very helpful to study the scriptures before such a prayer.

Such sincere praying reveals to us also the essence of building strong human relationships with other people, which leads us to the advanced-level, service initiative. If we are to truly serve others, it's important that we seek to understand *first,* before seeking to be understood. This takes empathy, or profound listening. We also learn to affirm to others their basic worth and their potential—in spite of what their behavior may be, not because of it. This represents the spirit of charity, which allows us to look on people as the Father does, with divine love and caring.

Basic Level— Personal Initiatives	Advanced Level— Enlarging Service Initiatives
1. Offer daily, listening prayers of faith.	1. Build strong human relationships through profound listening, affirming, caring service.

THE RESTORATION OF THE GOSPEL

WHOSE AM I?

CHAPTER 5

THE SECOND EVENT:
THE RESTORATION
OF THE GOSPEL

WHOSE AM I?

IN SEPTEMBER 1823, THREE YEARS AFTER the First Vision, Joseph Smith again poured out his heart in prayer to his Heavenly Father, seeking "forgiveness of all [his] sins and follies." In response to Joseph's prayer, the angel Moroni appeared to him and said that "God had a work for [him] to do." He explained that an ancient record engraved on gold plates was buried in the Hill Cumorah, near Joseph's home. He also said that Joseph was to translate the writings on these plates, which contained "the fulness of the everlasting Gospel" (Joseph Smith—History 1:29–35). Four years later, Moroni delivered the sacred record to the young prophet, who then translated it "by the gift and power of God" (*Teachings of the Prophet Joseph Smith,* 17) and published it to the world as the Book of Mormon, which is a second witness, with the Bible, of the Savior and his atoning sacrifice. Thus the gospel of Jesus Christ in its fullness and purity was restored to mankind.

The Gospel Defined

What is the gospel that was restored? The Lord told Joseph Smith, "Repent and be baptized, every one of you, for a remission of your sins; yea, be baptized even by water, and then cometh the baptism of fire and of the Holy Ghost. Behold, verily, verily, I say unto you, *this is my gospel;* and remember that they shall have faith in me or they can in nowise be saved" (D&C 33:11–12; emphasis added).

Faith in the atoning sacrifice of Jesus Christ is the central theme of the Book of Mormon and the central message of the Restoration. Just as the First Vision identifies *who* we are, the second transcendent event of the Restoration clarifies *whose* we are. The apostle Paul asked, "Know ye not that . . . ye are not your own? For ye are bought with a price" (1 Corinthians 6:19–20). The Book of Mormon explains, more clearly and powerfully than any other source, that we belong to the Savior because of the price he paid for us through his infinite atonement.

As King Benjamin said, "If you should render all the thanks and praise which your whole soul has power to possess, to that God who has created you, and has kept and preserved you, and has caused that ye should rejoice, and has granted that ye should live in peace one with another—I say unto you that if ye should serve him who has created you from the beginning, and is preserving you from day to day, by lending you breath, that ye may live and move and do according to your own will, and even supporting you from one moment to another—I say, if ye should serve him with all your whole souls yet ye would be unprofitable servants" (Mosiah 2:20–21).

Once we have entered mortality, how do we advance from where we are and achieve our full potential as children of God? Again, the answer is found in the Restoration, which reveals not only the *purpose* of our existence but also the *means* by which we can accomplish that purpose. The Savior said, "I am the way, the truth, and the life: no man cometh unto the Father, but by me" (John 14:6). Christ himself is the method, the means, the path. We are *his*.

Becoming Perfect in Christ

In the final chapter of the Book of Mormon, the prophet Moroni wrote, "Come unto Christ, and be perfected in him, and deny yourselves of all ungodliness; and if ye shall deny yourselves of all ungodliness, and love God with all your might, mind and strength, *then is his grace sufficient for you, that by his grace ye may be perfect in Christ;* and if by the grace of God ye are perfect in Christ, ye can in nowise deny the power of God" (Moroni 10:32; emphasis added). In other words, if we sincerely repent of our sins and trust in the Savior, his atonement compensates for our deficiencies, and we become "perfect in Christ"—not perfect *like* Christ, but perfect *in* Christ. That distinction is extremely important, and those who don't understand it often feel discouraged and hopeless. They feel ugly and sinful, and they may believe that they are not really celestial material at all.

The truth is that no one can become perfect *like* Christ in mortality. As Joseph Smith taught, "It will be a great while after you have passed through the veil before you will have learned [all the principles of exaltation]. It is not all to be comprehended in this world; it will be a great work to learn our salvation and exaltation even beyond the grave" (*Teachings of the Prophet Joseph Smith*, 348).

We will not become perfect *like* Christ in this life, but we can become perfect *in* Christ by entering into the holy covenant, the divine partnership, that he offers us. In a business partnership, if one partner possesses unlimited resources and assets, the other partner's limited resources and assets are made unlimited also. We could say the Savior is our senior partner. His infinite resources will cover our sins, compensate for the afflictions of our lives, and help us move toward eternal life. As long as we are true and faithful, as long as we stay in the covenant relationship, we are "perfect in Christ" and are saved *now*. And if we die while moving along the "strait and narrow path which leads to eternal life" (2 Nephi 31:18), we will remain in the path and arrive at our destination.

The Lord revealed to Joseph Smith, "Whatever principle of intelligence we attain unto in this life, it will rise with us in the resurrection. And if a person gains more knowledge and intelligence in this life through his diligence and obedience than another, he will have so much the advantage in the world to come" (D&C 130:18–19). Normally when we think of the word *advantage,* we think competitively—that is, of having advantage over others—but I'm convinced that's not what the Lord means here. I believe that the advantage referred to in this scripture means we are impelled ahead in our own growth and development. It's like getting onto the freeway of growth toward becoming more like our Savior. When a person has internalized the principles of the gospel, these principles become part of that person's nature, and he or she attains a new level of growth—a personal "advantage." I don't believe that the Lord makes comparisons as we do, and that in the Lord's plan everyone who runs the race faithfully will win. *Everyone* who internalizes gospel principles and lives by them will have so much more advantage in eternity.

The Savior is telling us continuously that we have the capacity to become celestial people. And what does the adversary say? "You'll never make it; you're always off track." But the Savior says, "You may get off track, but just keep coming back—back to your prayers, back to the scriptures, back to your meetings, back to your testimony. Keep staying faithful to your callings. Just keep coming back. I will be your advocate. Eventually you'll have eternal life." We should keep up hope. We shouldn't be so critical of ourselves. When we make mistakes, we should sincerely repent and take the sacrament to renew our covenants and remember our reliance on the Savior and his atoning sacrifice.

When people don't understand the Atonement, they often try to atone for their own sins. For instance, many young people have perfectionistic consciences, and when they do something wrong, they can be so hard on themselves that they commit a double wrong by refusing to accept the Savior's gift of healing and forgiveness. They slay themselves daily in a sense; they don't understand that Christ already atoned for their sins on the condition of repentance. "*He* was wounded for *our* transgressions, *he* was bruised for *our* iniquities . . . and with *his* stripes *we* are healed" (Isaiah 53:5; emphasis added).

One young woman told of how she learned to rely on the Atonement instead of her own strength:

> My roommates and I decided to start this diet so we could feel good about ourselves. It became a grueling routine that threw me back into habits that I had suffered from when I was younger. I started focusing on my faults and my weaknesses, and feeling that I was not good enough. I felt like I was inadequate for everything, and that I wasn't at the stage where I should be in my life. I thought I should be married, I should have kids, and I became frustrated and discouraged, thinking even more that something was wrong with me and that I was a failure. I kept thinking that I could do it on my own.
>
> I had gotten to the point where I was so discouraged with myself, I couldn't look in the mirror because I was so disgusted at what I saw. I couldn't look at pictures.

One day, I was getting ready and I had the thought that I should just purge and take care of it all. It was a scary thought to me, and I remember going up to my room and kneeling down and crying and telling Heavenly Father that I didn't know what to do anymore.

I talked to my sister, and she helped me make an appointment for a consultation with a counselor. I have never been as scared as I was that day. I almost got up and left, but I decided to stay. A gentleman came out to take me to a room, and we started talking. Ironically, this man wasn't even supposed to be interviewing me; it was supposed to be someone else, but he took me instead.

He first asked me what I thought of myself, and then what I thought God thought of me. He talked to me about allowing myself to be the way God wants me to be, and trying to see myself how He does, without imposing these standards or images of how I thought I should be.

He then sort of rebuked me and told me that I had to allow the Atonement to work in my life. "Right now you are trying to carry everything on your own," he said, "and you need to start working with Him instead of alone." He said that was what the Atonement was all about: allowing the Savior to work with me. I had weaknesses that everybody knew about, and I didn't want to deal with them. But instead of taking the opportunity to make my weaknesses stronger, I tried to shove them under a rug and tell Heavenly Father not to help me with them because they weren't really an issue. And in the process I separated myself from God.

I thought, "He is so right. I am not allowing this to work in my life right now." As soon as I realized that, it was like a huge weight being taken off my shoulders. I felt such a sense of hope and peace, and a realization of what I needed to do. I needed to apply the Atonement in my life. For the first time in almost a year, I really felt the peace that I had been longing for.

If it is the Savior's righteousness that saves us, then what do *we* offer? We offer our acceptance of him and our sincere willingness to do his will, and then we *do* his will. If we sometimes fall from the path, we get up and get back on again. While the Lord commands our perfection (for he can command nothing less), he allows for our imperfection. That is why repentance and the sacrament are part of the gospel covenant. As the Lord told Joseph Smith, "Seek ye earnestly the best gifts, always remembering for what they are given; for verily I say unto you, they are given for the benefit of those who love me and keep all my commandments, and *him that seeketh so to do*" (D&C 46:8–9; emphasis added).

What happens inside our minds and hearts when we start believing that Christ really is our Savior—here and now? I once saw a television show in which several people whose lives had been saved were brought together with those who had rescued them. They each told their story and talked about their feelings. One woman had been pinned under a car in a terrible accident, and a man had stopped to free her. Another woman had almost drowned in her vehicle, and her rescuer had dived into the freezing water, gotten his arms and hands into the car, and kept her head in a small pocket of air until additional help arrived. As hypothermia began to set in, the man feared he might die himself while trying to save the woman.

The television interviewer asked each of those who had been rescued, "How do feel about this person who saved your life?" Every one of them was very tearful and said something like this:

"I don't have words to describe how I feel. We were instantly bonded. I can never repay the debt I owe. I would do *anything* to help this person."

As I listened to these people I thought, What if we had that same feeling toward Christ every moment of our lives? What if, instead of thinking about salvation only in terms of some future state, we deeply believed that Christ is saving us *now*—and that if our lives ended today, we would inherit eternal life? I believe this kind of faith would profoundly affect our feelings toward the Savior and toward ourselves, and would increase our desire to forgive others' transgressions against us.

Christ—Our Advocate with Others

Normally we think of Christ as being our advocate with the Father: "Listen to him who is the advocate with the Father, who is pleading your cause before him—saying: Father, behold the sufferings and death of him who did no sin, in whom thou wast well pleased; behold the blood of thy Son which was shed, the blood of him whom thou gavest that thyself might be glorified; wherefore, Father, spare these my brethren that believe on my name, that they may come unto me and have everlasting life" (D&C 45:3–5).

That is one very significant part of his advocacy. Through his atonement, we can receive forgiveness for our sins and we do not have to suffer the pains of eternal suffering, because Christ has suffered those for us.

Christ is also our advocate with others. He can intervene in our relationships with others in exactly the same way he intervenes on our behalf with the Father. Thus, in many ways we do not have to suffer the pain, anguish, and sickness of people sinning against us, including prior generations.

First, his Spirit "lighteth every man that cometh into the

world" (John 1:9). It gives people a sense of right and wrong, and it blesses them with guilt when they violate that knowledge. Thus when people offend us, and we bless them in return, their guilty consciences represent Christ's advocacy of our cause. If we return evil for evil, we become our own advocates. In other words, when we rely on the arm of flesh, we're left to fight the battle ourselves, and inevitably we will retreat into a defensive posture and seek validation from others who agree with our position. But if we refuse to become angry and defensive, if we just smile deep within ourselves and bless those who trespass against us, the Savior is our advocate because his Spirit working in the heart of the aggressor provides a way for peace to result from the conflicts between people.

One man shared his conversion story with me. He thought the Mormons were a non-Christian American cult, so when the missionaries came to his door, he accused them of all kinds of evil. "I really raked them over the coals," he said. "But they treated me with such courtesy, such patience and respect, that it unnerved me. I continued to aggressively put them down, but they continued to return goodness. I could feel my conscience bothering me terribly, but I rationalized and told myself that these two were exceptions to the rule. I finally slammed the door. Then I went to the window and watched these two elders walk down the path and out into the street. One of them patted the other on the shoulder as if to say, 'Don't worry about it; let's keep going.' And I remembered that the Savior had said, 'By this shall all men know that ye are my disciples, if ye have love one to another' [John 13:35]. I couldn't stand it anymore. I ran to the front door, opened it up, and yelled out, 'Come back—I'll listen!'" He eventually joined the Church.

Christ also protects us *from* the sins of others. If we would repent, Christ becomes our defender against those who sin against us. He fills our lives with his calming, peacemaking way:

> For behold, I, God, have suffered these things for all, that they might not suffer if they would repent;
>
> But if they would not repent they must suffer even as I;
>
> Which suffering caused myself, even God, the greatest of all, to tremble because of pain, and to bleed at every pore, and to suffer both body and spirit—and would that I might not drink the bitter cup, and shrink—
>
> Nevertheless, glory be to the Father, and I partook and finished my preparations unto the children of men. (D&C 19:16–19.)

Seeing Others as Christ Sees Them

If we would repent—meaning to change our minds, to center our lives on Christ, to think and act as Christ thinks—then we will not suffer when others sin against us. If we think as Christ thinks, if we repent of our own sins and realize the tremendous gift extended to us through the Atonement, we become capable of extending that same gift to others. True repentance means truly coming to see others as Christ sees them and being able to extend the same generosity of forgiveness and abundance that he extends to us. The sins of others cannot truly hurt us with Christ as our advocate.

Years ago, I encountered a woman embittered toward her stake president because of some shady business dealing she believed he had engaged in. Her husband had come to peace with the situation and had decided not to sue. But she was still torn between wanting to be loyal to her leader and seeking revenge. As she gradually became aware of and full of Christ's light on the situation, not the light shed by her circumstances or what society would have her do, she changed her mind. Literally, her whole orientation toward the problem was reilluminated by the spirit of Christ, and she could see the problem as the Lord saw it. She started to see that there were two legitimate sides, two well-intentioned, well-meaning people acting in good faith. What started the process of reorientation or "re-seeing" was that she repented of her own sins, of her vindictiveness, of her desire for revenge. If she hadn't had this repenting experience to soften her heart and open her eyes, Christ could not have become the stake president's advocate with her, nor could Christ have become her Savior, saving her from being a victim of the supposed sins of other people against her and her husband.

Avoiding Taking Offense

The Savior said, "Blessed is he, whosoever shall not be offended in me" (Luke 7:23). I like to think that scripture means that if people have Christ within them, they have such an inner security that they are not vulnerable. They can't be offended from the outside. If they are, it's temporary, superficial, like a puff of wind that disturbs for a moment the tranquil surface of a lake. Oh, their ego might be hurt a little, but they soon get over it because they are nurtured and loved from the divine source, which love consumes any minor human attempt to offend. Essentially, people who are centered in Christ should not take offense. Their security isn't a function of how they are treated by others. It lies in a divine relationship with the Father through the Son.

Suppose someone has offended you. In fact, this person seems frequently to offend you and your children by his abrupt ways or the judgmental labels he places upon your family. Perhaps it is a neighbor, a fellow Church worker, an auxiliary teacher, or a high councilor assigned to your ward. It would really make no difference what the context was because the same principle would operate. That principle is that *when you consistently return kindness for unkindness,* patience in the face of impatience, good for evil, *you release the still, small voice inside of the other person to advocate your case,* and it will appeal to whatever good there is in that person.

Of course, there is no guarantee that this will result in a change in the offending person's behavior. As happens with many people in all kinds of situations, he may completely ignore the still, small voice. The point is that one of the main factors, perhaps the major one influencing whether he will listen to the voice or ignore it, will be your own behavior and attitude. If you are striving to follow Christ, you will seek to bless when being cursed, to forgive and forget, to move on in life with helpfulness and the eventual triumph of truth and righteousness. And such a pattern arouses enticings to righteousness in the consciences of all those around you, representing an "upward temptation." Again, in effect, you have the Savior as your advocate.

When Christ is our partner in the gospel covenant, he becomes our champion and our advocate. We don't need then to protect ourselves against other people by judgment, categorization, sarcasm, or criticism. Our security doesn't come from how others treat us; it comes from the relationship we have with the Father through our Savior. This is what enables us to return kindness for unkindness, to love our enemies, to bless those who curse us, and to pray for those who speak evil against us falsely. Remember it isn't the bite of the poisonous snake that does the greatest harm. It's chasing the snake that drives the poison to the heart.

The Promise of Eternal Life

Elder Bruce R. McConkie clearly stated the Lord's promise to members of the Church who remain true to their covenant relationship with Him:

All the faithful Saints, all of those who have endured to the end, depart this life with the absolute guarantee of eternal life.

There is no equivocation, no doubt, no uncertainty in our minds. Those who have been true and faithful in this life will not fall by the wayside in the life to come. If they keep their covenants here and now and depart this life firm and true in the testimony of our blessed Lord, they shall come forth with an inheritance of eternal life.

We do not mean to say that those who die in the Lord, and who are true and faithful in this life, must be perfect in all things when they go into the next sphere of existence. There was only one perfect man—the Lord Jesus whose Father was God. . . .

But what we are saying is that when the saints of God chart a course of righteousness, when they gain sure testimonies of the truth and divinity of the Lord's work, when they keep the commandments, when they overcome the world, when they put first in their lives the things of God's kingdom: when they do all these things, and then depart this life—though they have not yet become perfect—they shall nonetheless gain eternal life in our Father's kingdom; and eventually they shall be perfect as God their Father and Christ His Son are perfect ("The Dead Who Die in the Lord," *Ensign,* November 1976, 105–6).

Just think of all the people you know in the Church who are regularly covenanting and trying to be better and also sincerely trying to serve people on both sides of the veil. Think of all their peculiarities and idiosyncrasies, their weaknesses and limitations. But now think of them as being perfect in Christ; think of how his perfection is compensating for their weaknesses and limitations and how they are truly on the path to eternal life.

Many times when I've attended funerals and listened to the lofty eulogies of people's lives and virtues, I have wondered if those people were really as good as they were being described. I've even heard expressions of the assurance that these people were taken into heaven, that they would be together with their loved ones as part of the eternal family, which, of course, means exaltation and eternal life in the celestial kingdom. And I have often thought, "How can they be so sure?"

I understood better as I witnessed the passing away of my sister Marilyn from a wasting cancer. She had just been released as the ward Relief Society president because of her drastically failing health, but she was consumed by her desire to bless her posterity through her death by teaching them how to die and therefore, in a sense, how to live for purpose and meaning and each other's happiness. She was extremely close to her children and grandchildren and cared for them so constantly in her prayers and her daily actions that she could hardly do anything without thinking of them. Right at the end, although she was in agony, she was full of good humor, and her consciousness was inside the hearts and heads of her loved ones. Each one in turn, whether a child or a grandchild, she attempted to bless, to teach, to testify to, to express love to.

I was to speak at the funeral, and as I prepared my talk, I thought of this scripture: "If your eye be single to my glory, your whole bodies shall be filled with light, . . . and that body which is filled with light comprehendeth all things" (D&C 88:67). I thought, "What is God's glory? It's to bring to pass the immortality and eternal life of man. What is Marilyn's focus and purpose? It is God's glory." I found myself thinking of her as a perfect person.

At that time I hadn't made clearly the distinction between being perfect in Christ and being perfect like Christ, but as I think back on it now, I can clearly see that Marilyn was perfect in Christ. She, like the rest of us, had much growth and development to go through before becoming perfect like Christ. Nevertheless, the spirit of grace, the spirit of the Atonement and of Christ's righteousness compensated for her weaknesses and supplied the lens through which I saw her, so I saw her as a perfect person. I could not think of her weaknesses or faults at all. They were totally subsumed in the spirit of grace and charity. I saw her as one whose eye was single to the glory of God right to the end of her life, to the very last breath of mortality. Her feet were firmly planted on the path leading to eternal life. This was all confirmed during the funeral within me and many others, and I have no doubt that she is still on that path, doing work for her loved ones and many others.

I wish I'd understood the distinction between being perfect *in* Christ and being perfect *like* Christ a long time ago. I would have perceived things differently—other people, myself, and all the processes of life. To some degree I have been influenced by a strong culture that defines salvation as a kind of human perfection, teaching that even though we believe in the Atonement, we basically save ourselves through our good works.

Justice, Mercy, or Repentance unto Baptism

Most of the world has a justice paradigm: an eye for an eye, get what's coming to you, pull yourself up by your own bootstraps. Most of Christianity has a mercy paradigm, sometimes referred to as "cheap grace": sincerely and believingly acknowledge Christ as your Savior, and you're saved, regardless of your later behavior. I feel that often Latter-day Saints, in an effort to avoid the cheap grace approach, fall into the trap of a justice paradigm and have a hard time fully accepting Christ's atoning sacrifice for them personally. We need to be reminded that the restored gospel has a "*repentance* unto baptism" paradigm: exercise faith in Christ, do your very best, cultivate a broken heart and a contrite spirit, and repent constantly of mistakes and sins in order to be baptized (renewed at sacrament) and to claim the blessings of the Atonement, so that you can have the sense of being perfect *in* Christ and can then get on the pathway to becoming perfect *like* Christ.

What do we mean when we say "the spirits of just men made perfect?" (D&C 76:69; Hebrews 12:23). "Just" men and women are not perfect people. They are imperfect people who have been justified through the atonement of Christ, who have been made perfect *in* Christ, and they are still on the path to becoming perfect *like* Christ. Their perfection, their wholeness, their completeness comes from God's righteousness, not theirs, even though they were sufficiently obedient and diligent—that is, righteous in receiving God's righteousness through the Atonement.

Since I have come to understand the difference between being perfect *in* Christ and being perfect *like* Christ, I have begun to see people differently, to see them as celestial people, to be less judgmental about personality weaknesses, psychological hang-ups, or behavior that is not Christlike. It has made me want to covenant with deeper sincerity and humility. It has made me more grateful for the Atonement, not less. It has made me want to be better and do more rather than be contented and rest on my laurels. I find myself continually reinventing my life and wanting to serve in entirely new ways. I still see many of my weaknesses and limitations, and I want to work on those and use more of the spiritual, *enabling* powers and gifts and the Atonement in overcoming them.

No one is perfect. But we can be perfect in Christ and eventually perfect like Christ. We can understand either one of those two ideas only by thinking about both ideas simultaneously. Otherwise we'd face the dangers of complacency on the one hand and a feeling of hopeless imperfection on the other. The key to experiencing both of them simultaneously is to be focused on blessing someone else's life. Then the Lord will use us in his way, may even prune us so we will bring forth more fruit (John 15:1–5), and he will give us his *enabling* Spirit, his gifts, and his blessings to do whatever it takes to bless and serve another person.

Receiving the Atonement through Personal Sacrifice

Elder Bruce C. Hafen teaches that the Savior accomplished essentially three things through his atoning sacrifice. First, he provided for the remission of our sins if we repent, enabling us to be justified or "perfect in Christ." Second, he compensated for the mistakes we unknowingly commit, the sicknesses we experience, the psychic and social traumas caused by mistreatment or even terrible abuse during our childhood, and so forth. He compensated for all of these things. And third, he facilitated the process by which we can be sanctified and eventually become perfect *like* Christ (see *The Broken Heart,* 41).

Even those who have suffered from profound injustice and felt deeply misunderstood can find infinite understanding in Jesus Christ. Because his love and his atonement go deeper than all of our traumas, he is the ultimate source of healing. When he is our true foundation, he sustains any blow, no matter how piercing or blinding or powerful.

One woman writes:

> I always felt the Atonement was for sin. I never had
> thought, ever, about it being for burdens or for heartache.
> And even when I asked the Lord to take a problem from
> me, the word *atonement* didn't come into my mind. My
> thinking was more along the lines of, "Take this from me,
> take care of it, I don't want it. I can't deal with it any-
> more."
>
> But I've come to realize, after several experiences,
> what has happened when I have accepted the Savior's
> atonement for my trials. Literally everything I have felt,
> it was as if he had felt it before. I learned to believe that
> he had carried this for me already, so why was I carrying
> it?
>
> I didn't realize how unhappy I must have looked
> before, because I can't tell you how many people could
> see the change. They would come up to me and say, "You
> look so much better—what have you done?" Well, I
> knew what I had done: I had gotten rid of all the burden.

Receiving by Sacrifice

What must we do to receive the supernal gift of the
Atonement? We will discuss that question more fully in the next
chapter, but at this point I would suggest that the Savior's sacrifice
takes effect in our lives when we offer sacrifice to him. What sacrifice does the Lord want from us? He told Joseph Smith, "Thou
shalt offer a sacrifice unto the Lord thy God in righteousness,
even that of a broken heart and a contrite spirit" (D&C 59:8). In
Old Testament times, the Lord required the sacrifice of rams and
bullocks and doves, which, as the angel said to Adam, were "a

similitude of the sacrifice of the Only Begotten of the Father, which is full of grace and truth" (Moses 5:7). Now that the Savior's sacrifice has been completed, however, the Lord no longer requires the sacrifice of animals; instead, he wants our innermost selves, with nothing held back: "All . . . who know their hearts are honest, and are broken, and their spirits contrite, and are willing to observe their covenants by sacrifice—yea, every sacrifice which I, the Lord, shall command—they are accepted of me" (D&C 97:8).

And the Lord does ask for other kinds of sacrifice throughout our lives. We are willing to make these other sacrifices because of our overriding sacrifice of a broken heart and a contrite spirit. Sometimes the Lord requires sacrifice on a very physical level: praying when we're tired, fasting when we're hungry, paying tithes and offerings, and so forth. This level of sacrifice is hard for many people, and I believe that those who make such sacrifices are compensated by God with a greater knowledge of him and of themselves.

"You learn to love by loving others," one woman told me who had experienced this for herself. "When you start to love and care for Heavenly Father's sheep and you start making that sacrifice, you realize the sacrifices that have been made for you. Then you understand the Atonement. Once, after I went to serve a handicapped brother in our ward, I had to lie down for three hours when I got home because I was all hunched over from trying to take care of his needs. I knew that I had given in a way that my Savior would give to me. That man could not give back to me in any way. And I could never give back to the Savior what he has given me, by forgiving me, by coming to the earth and going through his experience and being the role model that he was, setting the example."

The Uttermost Farthing

Another kind of sacrifice is to seek to repair relationships that we may have damaged by our imperfect behavior. Consider the Savior's teaching from the Sermon on the Mount: "Agree with thine adversary quickly, whiles thou art in the way with him; lest at any time the adversary deliver thee to the judge, and the judge deliver thee to the officer, and thou be cast into prison. Verily I say unto thee, Thou shalt by no means come out thence, till thou hast paid the uttermost farthing" (Matthew 5:25–26).

Sometimes in our hearts we know that we have crossed the sensitive line and hurt or insulted or offended another person. We may have felt justified at the time—the person may have "deserved" this treatment—but from the Savior's standards as given in the Sermon on the Mount, we learn that we are not to react to the treatment of others but rather to act from within, based on his divine value system. We are to overcome evil with good instead of paying it off.

Therefore, when we hurt other people, we should go to them and acknowledge it and seek their forgiveness. This, in my opinion, is paying the uttermost farthing, if it comes out of our heart and is not used merely as a manipulative technique.

I found the efficacy of this principle in my own labor with people who were low in desire and irresponsible in performance. I remember one person who was neither completely rebellious nor very enthusiastic. He would just barely go along. I had him labeled thus in my mind, and for a number of months, every time I saw his face and name on organization charts, I would think of him in this way. In the periodic reviews, even though on the surface I would appear interested, under it all I had him labeled and categorized in my mind.

Eventually I reached the point where I knew I had to take

some initiative myself and do something else that might help him "get on fire." He began to open up, saying something like, "Dr. Covey, I know you have a lot of good ideas and advice for me, but could you kind of listen to what I feel like and what my problems are and help me from there?" I did what I could at the time, but my inability to remove myself from the label I had about him was so set that I needed more time to prepare. In the intervening time I looked introspectively at myself and became aware of how I had labeled him and how this label had tended to be a self-fulfilling prophecy. People tend to become like we treat them or like we believe them to be—or we may simply interpret the data of our experiences with them in a way that proves our label.

I decided I needed to "pay the uttermost farthing," to use the Savior's expression. I went to this young man, opened up what I believed had happened and how I had played my role in contributing to this situation, and sought his forgiveness. He broke down and acknowledged his role in things also. He too paid the uttermost farthing, in a sense. Our relationship began on a new basis at step one, but for the first time it was thoroughly honest. Both of us began to build with each other, and he would use me from time to time as a sounding board to thrash out a lot of his feelings, both negative and positive. Gradually he "came to himself" (see Luke 15:17) and began to build internal controls; then he performed magnificently in achieving the results that came with his position, and he became supremely happy in his work.

With my own children I have needed to use this principle. I have sometimes crossed over the sensitive line and disciplined out of an angry mood, and I knew I had wounded their feelings. My pride, for a while, has often kept me from paying the uttermost farthing, but eventually I knew I must swallow my pride and specifically admit how I had offended, then express my sorrow and seek forgiveness.

What happens when a person pays the uttermost farthing? Assume, to begin with, that relationships are hurt and strained and that you are at least partly responsible. If you merely try to be better, without confessing and asking forgiveness, the other person will still be suspicious. She has been hurt and wounded, and therefore her guard is up. She will be defensive and suspicious of your new behavior, your "kind face," wondering what might happen next. Your improved behavior and manner do not change her distrustful perception. Nothing you can do will change it, because you are behind bars and walls in a prison of her own making (in her mind). The bars and walls are the mental and emotional labels that she has put upon you and that give her some feeling of security (in knowing not to expect much from you). When we expect nothing, we're never disappointed.

Only by a complete, full, and specific acknowledgment of your own failings will you pay the uttermost farthing. This same principle applies in seeking the Lord's forgiveness. We must hold nothing back—must hide nothing—and must surrender completely and totally to his will, his way, and his power.

Giving Away Our Sins

On another level of sacrifice, we must *repent* of all of our sins. As the father of King Lamoni said, "O God, Aaron hath told me that there is a God; and if there is a God, and if thou art God, wilt thou make thyself known unto me, and *I will give away all my sins to know thee*" (Alma 22:18; emphasis added).

When we repent, we give up our deeply ingrained habits and lifestyles that are in violation of God's commandments. The Savior said, "By this ye may know if a man repenteth of his sins—

behold, he will confess them and forsake them" (D&C 58:43). But in reality, confessing and forsaking our sins are not repentance—they are the *fruits* of repentance. True repentance is much more than a change in behavior; it is the shifting of our character orientation. It is the changing of our minds, the recentering of our lives, the complete giving of our hearts to Christ and his service. Otherwise we may repent of our sins but not of our sinning.

How do we know that the confession we have made in repentance has been accepted? That is an important question, because the less we get our sense of worth from the Savior, the more our sins will cause guilt, and we'll continue to blame ourselves. But if we feel a hope in Christ, we will work sincerely with a broken heart and contrite spirit to move beyond our sins. The spirit of peace will come, and we will know that our sins have been forgiven and forgotten. The Lord says he will "remember them no more" (D&C 58:42), and neither will we, in the sense that they will no longer torture us with self-hatred and low self-worth. What is really exciting about this is what it does to our spirits when we feel this relationship and how it affects our relationship with others. After we have truly repented and been forgiven, we no longer feel the compulsion to judge others or to be offended.

Judge Not

The Savior said, "Judge not, that ye be not judged" (Matthew 7:1). We are not only wrong to judge others but we are also incompetent to do so, because we are often totally without understanding of the many, many factors that help to formulate the point of view that directly affects a person's behavior.

"Why beholdest thou the mote that is in thy brother's eye," asked the Savior, "but considerest not the beam that is in thine own eye? Or how wilt thou say to thy brother, Let me pull out the mote out of thine eye; and, behold, a beam is in thine own eye? Thou hypocrite, first cast out the beam out of thine own eye; and then shalt thou see clearly to cast out the mote out of thy brother's eye" (Matthew 7:3–5).

Great truths are given to us here. First, there is a strong, almost universal tendency to find the fault in another—that is, the mote that is in our brother's eye. Second, when we focus on this mote—the other person's fault—we don't focus on the beam or fault in our own life. Third, in this spirit we often try to correct another. It doesn't work. We may have a correct opinion, but our spirit is wrong. Then we hurt, reject, offend, and threaten. Spirit, or attitude, communicates far more powerfully than opinions or gilded words. Fourth, because of the beam in our own eye, we are unable to see clearly. Our judgment or opinion may be entirely wrong. We may be merely projecting our own weaknesses and calling them the other person's problems. We may mistake introspection for observation. Perhaps that is what Paul meant when he said, "Therefore thou art inexcusable, O man, whosoever thou art that judgest: for wherein thou judgest another, thou condemnest thyself; for thou that judgest doest the same things" (Romans 2:1).

How widespread is this mote/beam sickness! To some degree it afflicts all of us. We might be terribly concerned about the various injustices in the nation, or in an institution, but how just are we in rearing our own children? Is our discipline consistent, based on well-established and well-communicated rules, or is it based on the mood of the moment? Are we upset with the hypocrisy of others? Do we live what we profess?

It is clear why we are unsuited to pass judgment on each

other. Fortunately, the Lord relieves us of this burden. Joseph Smith gave us a better understanding of how the *Lord* judges:

> While one portion of the human race is judging and condemning the other without mercy, the Great Parent of the universe looks upon the whole of the human family with a fatherly care and paternal regard; He views them as His offspring, and without any of those contracted feelings that influence the children of men, causes "His sun to rise on the evil and on the good, and sendeth rain on the just and on the unjust." He holds the reins of judgment in His hands; He is a wise Lawgiver, and will judge all men, not according to the narrow, contracted notions of men, but, "according to the deeds done in the body whether they be good or evil" (*History of the Church*, 4:595–96).

Forgive to Receive Forgiveness

Another way of forgoing judgment is to *forgive* those who have trespassed against us. This is even deeper than behavioral repentance, and it flows naturally from having a broken heart and a contrite spirit. When we forgive those who sin against us, especially when they are unrepentant, we are giving grace. The scriptures tell us we "shall receive grace for grace" (D&C 93:20), and I believe that one interpretation of that passage suggests that we can *receive* grace only as we *give* grace. Imagine the purification that takes place in a person's soul when he or she follows the example of Christ as he suffered on the cross: "Father, forgive them; for they know not what they do" (Luke 23:34). Imagine the growth and the reservoir of spiritual power that opens to a person who reaches that level of sacrifice!

Forgiving others forges a bond between us that enhances our love. As the Savior said of the woman who washed his feet, "Her sins, which are many, are forgiven; for she loved much: but to whom little is forgiven, the same loveth little" (Luke 7:47). Forgiveness and love go hand in hand, both in our relationships with God and in our interactions with other people.

I've thought a lot about empathy, which is understanding someone else from that person's frame of reference. In literally hundreds of settings over the years, I have found this the most challenging and difficult of tasks. For one thing, it takes great internal security to risk that level of openness. Sympathy is relatively easy compared to empathy, because in sympathy you have had the experience and can therefore relate to what the other person is going through. But in empathy, whether you have had the experience or not, you figuratively leave your consciousness and enter the consciousness of another so that you understand the other person intellectually and emotionally. The atonement of Christ was the greatest expression of empathy, because even though the Savior never sinned, he so empathized with us as to know our sins and suffer for them, both in body and spirit.

However, his suffering has no force unless we repent, which includes our suffering. As President Spencer W. Kimball said, "Repentance means suffering. If a person hasn't suffered, he hasn't repented" (*The Teachings of Spencer W. Kimball,* 99; see also 88). But the suffering of repentance is different in kind from suffering without repentance. When we repent, the Savior suffers for our sins, and we suffer in changing our lives, our thinking, our hearts—in going through profound, godly sorrow. That is part of our progression along the path.

Becoming Perfect Like Christ

The restoration of the gospel through the Book of Mormon enables us to understand and use the enabling power of the Atonement, making it possible for us to become perfect *in* Christ, or *justified*. But it also shows us the way to reach our ultimate goal, which is to become perfect *like* Christ, or *sanctified*.

During his mortal ministry, Christ commanded his disciples, "Be . . . perfect, even as your Father which is in heaven is perfect" (Matthew 5:48). But after his resurrection he said, "I would that ye should be perfect *even as I,* or your Father who is in heaven is perfect" (3 Nephi 12:48; emphasis added). What accounts for the difference between these two statements? The scriptures tell us that "he received not of the fulness at first, but continued from grace to grace, until he received a fulness; . . . and the glory of the Father was with him, for he dwelt in him" (D&C 93:13, 17). In other words, he grew to become like his Father.

Most people have such a negative concept of who they are that their true capacity is almost lost. But with Christ there was no straying at all. He "descended below all things" (D&C 88:6), yet he lived a pure and sinless life, even in the face of extreme temptation. This allowed the Father's spirit to develop within him to such an extent that the full potential of his divine nature was released.

Elohim is the father of our spirit bodies, and Christ can become the father of the mind and heart—the way we see life, the way we interpret life, the way we deal with life. As King Benjamin told his people, "Because of the covenant which ye have made ye shall be called the children of Christ, his sons, and his daughters; for behold, this day he hath spiritually begotten you; for ye say that your hearts are changed through faith on his name; therefore, ye are born of him and have become his sons and his daughters" (Mosiah 5:7).

We need to let the Savior's mind become our mind, and his spirit our spirit. As we prayerfully examine his life, visualizing the circumstances in which he served and carefully studying his habits, his decisions, and his actions, we will learn to identify with him to the point that we no longer have to look to other people as our models. As King Benjamin's people experienced, we will have "no more disposition to do evil, but to do good continually" (Mosiah 5:2).

The Savior is more than a model; he is also willing to be our *mentor*. A mentor is a model with whom we have a relationship—someone who is our advocate. A mentor is someone who cares for us, takes a personal interest in our growth and development, and champions us. Christ is our elder brother; we are members of the same family. If we accept him as our mentor, we have a relationship with him, and he enables us to have a relationship with our Heavenly Father. How can we do that? By entering into his covenant and constantly returning to it, and by looking into our own hearts to see what we need to do. The Lord will tell us—is continually telling us, if we will listen—through his Spirit, the Holy Ghost, by which he will lead us upward as well as onward through greater levels of intelligence and consciousness until we see as he sees and know as he knows. The Lord told Joseph Smith that those who dwell in the Father's presence "see as they are seen, and know as they are known, having received of his fulness and of his grace" (D&C 76:94; see also 1 Corinthians 13:12).

The social mirror imposes on us a straitjacket of dependency and jealousy and scarcity. But the Savior broke this mirror. If we will accept him as our mentor, he becomes the father of our minds, the father of our hearts. Then, like him, we can obtain—

line upon line, precept upon precept—the fullness of the Father. If we truly receive him, through our faithfulness to the principles and ordinances of the gospel, his Atonement meets the demands of justice, and he gives us the gift of the Holy Ghost. Through that gift, our consciousness gradually expands until we too become partakers of the divine nature.

The word *atonement* actually means "at-one-ment." I believe that Christ enables us to become one with ourselves, one with other people, and one with God. His atoning sacrifice overcomes the effects of spiritual death as we repent of our sins, and thus we can eventually return to the presence of our Heavenly Father. The Savior also brings unity and harmony between people who have broken hearts and contrite spirits. And as we give ourselves to him, he enables us to be unified, integrated, and reconciled with our true celestial identity.

Internalizing the Second Event

It seems to me that there is no subject we should study more seriously than the Atonement. And the most effective way to gain an understanding of this doctrine is to study the Book of Mormon, because almost every page of it teaches us about Jesus Christ and his gospel. That is why Joseph Smith said that "the Book of Mormon [is] the most correct of any book on earth, and the keystone of our religion, and a man [can] get nearer to God by abiding by its precepts, than by any other book" (*Teachings of the Prophet Joseph Smith,* 194).

The personal initiative for the second event is to ponder the scriptures daily, to feast on the words and love of Jesus Christ. Christ himself said that he was the bread of life. In the Lord's prayer, he used the expression "Give us this day our daily bread." To me, this refers not just to physical sustenance; it could also be interpreted, "Give us this day our Savior and Redeemer and his atoning sacrifice."

We should feast daily on the words of Christ in the Book of Mormon. It's like gathering manna every day and letting the wisdom of heaven distill upon our minds and hearts. It's also like putting on a pair of glasses. We see *everything* through the lens of whatever we choose to put at the center of our lives, and the Book of Mormon helps us become Christ-centered because it answers the question, "Whose am I?"

Understanding and internalizing the Atonement is the key to experiencing the second transcendent event of the Restoration on a personal level. If we want to have that experience—or help others do so—we must devote ourselves to in-depth study and pondering over many weeks and months until we are gradually soaked in the doctrines of the Atonement and begin to see all of life through it. Only constant and prayerful effort and the influence of the Spirit can enable the finite mind to begin to comprehend the infinite and tap into its power. Daily scripture study, then, becomes the basic personal initiative for this second event.

During my second mission I came to realize, more than ever before, the transcendent importance of the Atonement. I could see how this supreme sacrifice gave power and efficacy to every gospel principle, teaching, law, and ordinance. In my desire to increase my understanding of it, particularly to more fully understand the nature and extent of the divine love that motivated it, I prayerfully studied the scriptures on this matter for several months. I was not expecting any sudden, unusual manifestation, but I found increased enlightenment and understanding, and my soul was satisfied. Still, I continued with my studying and pondering and asking, finding that the more I knew and felt, the more light I desired.

Returning home from a mission tour after several days away, I was hurrying so I could see my two daughters before they went to bed. I dashed upstairs to their bedroom the minute I pulled in, not even stopping to unpack the car, but they were fast asleep. My wife was on a Relief Society assignment, and I was alone with my thoughts and feelings. I was surprised to sense that I was not disappointed after such an effort but rather felt full of spiritual desire. Even now I can't describe the nature of this desire, except to say that I enjoyed the solitude and spirit in the girls' room and the beautiful, tranquil scene outside. I wanted to stay there, to look at them in their cots—so peaceful and lovely. The whole mission home seemed unusually quiet. I reveled in the peace and the scene and the feeling and wanted to stay there.

I did stay. For a long time I sat and looked and felt. I felt to pray. I felt to pray for my daughters and even blessed them in their sleep. I envisioned those two little girls returning and serving missions in Ireland at a future time (which they both eventually did).

These feelings of gratitude and love continued until I couldn't express them anymore. Suffice it to say that the feeling of love began to spread out from that room to everyone who lived or worked in the mission home, then to all the missionaries, then to the Saints in Ireland, and eventually to all the people of Ireland. This love seemed to comprehend everyone individually. I simply have no words to describe it. But I loved everybody as I had never loved before, or perhaps since, and this love seemed to possess the characteristic of knowledge.

I came to feel that I was tasting a part of the kind of love that lay behind the Atonement. I felt it was charity, the pure love of Christ, and that such a supernal love was a gift of God. I felt it was—in part, at least—an answer to my prayers for an understanding of the Atonement. Moroni 7:48 became precious to me: "Wherefore, my beloved brethren, pray unto the Father with all the energy of heart, that ye may be filled with this love, which he hath bestowed upon all who are true followers of his Son, Jesus Christ; that ye may become the sons of God; that when he shall appear we shall be like him, for we shall see him as he is; that we may have this hope; that we may be purified even as he is pure."

For many days the spirit of that experience stayed with me without any conscious effort on my part. And to this day I vividly remember the scene and the feeling. It has given to me a love standard and a realization that charity is truly a *gift* of God. I have hesitated to share such a personal experience, but I have felt to do so in love and as my personal testimony of the Atonement and the power of love as life's central motivation.

As we come to understand and internalize the Savior's atoning sacrifice, we can begin to lead our family members and others to him. Hence, the advanced service initiative is to teach and testify of Christ by the power of the Holy Spirit. But we must remember that people cannot personally experience the second event of the Restoration until they have experienced the first event. Only when they have a deep conviction of their real identity and their celestial potential can they feel the inner security to turn to the Lord and align their souls with the Atonement. Yet, in another sense, the first and second events are perfectly interwoven in teaching us of our true identity and relationship with the Father, the Son, and the Holy Ghost.

If we want to help people obtain hope in Christ, we must exercise great empathy and patience, and we must continually affirm that they are of infinite worth. We must be faithful to them, as the Savior himself would be. They must sense that we have integrity. The key to influencing others to come unto Christ is in offering an example of absolute constancy under stress. We are like midwives in the "second birth" process, and for many people it's a painful struggle to overcome personal habits and offer up the sacrifice of a broken heart and a contrite spirit. As we help them do so, they must know that we will not abort the process— no matter what happens.

Basic Level— Personal Initiatives	Advanced Level— Enlarging Service Initiatives
1. Offer daily, listening prayers of faith.	1. Build strong human relationships through profound listening, affirming, and caring service.
2. Ponder the scriptures daily to feast on the words and love of Jesus Christ. ("Give us this day our daily bread.")	2. Teach and testify, by the Spirit, of Christ and his atoning sacrifice.

THE RESTORATION
OF THE PRIESTHOOD

HOW CAN I RECEIVE CHRIST?

CHAPTER 6

THE THIRD EVENT: THE RESTORATION OF THE PRIESTHOOD

HOW CAN I RECEIVE CHRIST?

WHILE TRANSLATING THE BOOK OF MORMON, Joseph Smith and Oliver Cowdery learned that people must be baptized for the remission of their sins. So in May 1829, they went into the woods, near Harmony, Pennsylvania, and asked the Lord about baptism. In response to their prayer, John the Baptist appeared to them, ordained them to the Aaronic Priesthood, and commanded them to baptize each other. Not long afterward, Peter, James, and John appeared and ordained Joseph and Oliver to the Melchizedek Priesthood.

The restoration of the priesthood answers the question "How can we receive Christ's gospel and the blessings of his atonement?" Specifically, the priesthood is the power of God delegated to his worthy male children to "preach the Gospel and administer in the ordinances thereof" (Article of Faith 5), and it is by receiving these sacred *ordinances* that we enter into the gospel covenant. Through this means, the Atonement takes effect in our lives so that we can be sanctified. Thus the ordinances of the priesthood enable us to get onto the path of eternal life.

It's the ordinances that separate celestial activity from terrestrial activity. Through them, we accomplish the mission of the Church. We proclaim the gospel by bringing people to baptism, we perfect the Saints by bringing them to the sacrament and to the temple, and we redeem the dead by performing vicarious ordinances in their behalf. These are celestial *works* because they orient a person to God and enable his soul to be saved and perfected.

Of course, we should also do many good *works* on a terrestrial level by serving the physical, emotional, intellectual, psychological, and spiritual needs of other people. If we study the Savior's life, we can see that it was filled with good works of this kind. He blessed and comforted and healed many people, and the apostle Peter said that he "went about doing good" (Acts 10:38). But his ultimate purpose was to lead people to the ordinances of the gospel, because without these they are not deeply changed in their nature. As Joseph Smith taught, "Being born again comes by the Spirit of God through ordinances" (*Teachings of the Prophet Joseph Smith,* 162).

The administering of the ordinances of the kingdom—a celestial activity—and the establishment of God's kingdom required a restoration of sacred priesthood power and authority. Of this Elder Bruce R. McConkie taught:

> This Priesthood of Melchizedek is the highest and holiest order given to mortals now or ever. It includes now, and has always included, the power and authority of the holy apostleship.
>
> With it the struggling mortals who will soon, by divine command, organize anew the Church and

kingdom of God on earth, receive certain keys of almost infinite import.

They receive the keys of the kingdom by virtue of which they are empowered to organize, preside over, govern, and regulate the kingdom of God on earth, which is The Church of Jesus Christ of Latter-day Saints.

They also receive the keys of the dispensation of the fulness of times, that glorious age of restoration and refreshment in which God designs to gather all things in one in Christ; that age of revelation and gifts and miracles in which he will bring to pass the restitution of all things spoken by the mouths of all the holy prophets since the world began. (See D&C 27:12–13; D&C 81:2.) ("The Keys of the Kingdom," *Ensign,* May 1983, 21).

The Integrating Power of Covenant Making

It's inspiring to see a new governmental official, particularly the president of a country, take the oath of office. It's inspiring to watch new doctors take the Hippocratic Oath. I have seen people in many situations struggle with whether or not to sign a particular paper or to make a particular promise through that signature.

Ordinances are like this, only more. Ordinances are not social rituals; they aren't artificial hoops that we have to jump through to join the Church or to renew our commitments weekly. When we participate in an ordinance, we are declaring our deep "Yes" to the Lord's commandment. This is very personal on a spiritual level, regardless of the cultural and institutional implications.

The ordinances of the priesthood actually bind us to the Lord. Through these ordinances we enter into a *covenant,* which is a two-way promise. A covenant is different from a commitment. When we make a commitment, we promise that we will do a certain thing. But when we enter into a covenant with God, we make a promise to him and he also makes a promise to us. If we remain true to our promise, he promises that we will have peace in this life and inherit eternal life in his presence.

According to the Book of Mormon, "many covenants of the Lord" were taken out of the Bible after it was originally written (1 Nephi 13:26; see verses 19–40). If Satan could destroy covenant making, he would be able to remove the plan given in mortality to perfect the human soul. That's one of the reasons why the priesthood was a central part of the Restoration. The covenants of the gospel are administered through priesthood ordinances, and thus the ordinances are the key to our becoming perfect in Christ. The Book of Mormon, too, teaches us of the covenants that were removed from the Bible. And the Doctrine and Covenants not only puts them back in but is also the modern-day manifestation of the power to administer them.

The power in such a covenant is illustrated in one convert's memory of his baptism:

> I have a tender feeling about my baptism. It was very special, very spiritual—just a really sweet, pure experience. I could literally feel that things in my past were gone, and that Father in Heaven was not looking at those any longer. There was a new, renewed feeling at that time.
>
> We partake of the sacrament to renew our covenants, and I think it gives you the same type of feeling that you feel when you're baptized. It's not as strong as when I was baptized, but still I have that feeling that I have an opportunity to confess my sins and to repent—to wipe the slate clean.

A covenant requires that we turn our whole souls to the Lord. It can't be a superficial, mechanical, compartmentalized experience; we can't do it to impress someone else or to satisfy someone that we've done our duty. We must align our entire selves with Christ. When I enter into such a covenant, I completely unify my mind, my will, my loyalty, and my enthusiasm. I marshal all of my mental, emotional, and spiritual resources to say, "I promise. My mind is made up." My belief system, my habit system, my intuition, and every part of my nature essentially comes together and says, "I will." When that takes place, heaven also moves, and God commits and covenants with me. Thus I can become completely integrated, both with my own nature and with heaven.

Make and Keep a Promise

Many times people have asked me, "What is one thing I can do to really help me get back on the gospel path?" I often say to them, "Make and keep a promise. Start small, but make a promise and keep it. After you've done that, make and keep larger and larger promises until you're able to witness to God that you're willing to take upon yourself the name of his Son, and always remember him and keep his commandments, so that you may always have his Spirit to be with you."

To make up one's mind is not an easy thing. The Savior asked those who followed him, "Which of you, intending to build a tower, sitteth not down first, and counteth the cost, whether he have sufficient to finish it?" He then explained the extent of the commitment he requires of us: "Whosoever . . . forsaketh not all that he hath, he cannot be my disciple" (Luke 14:28, 33). To be a true disciple, a person must be willing to subordinate everyone and everything to Christ—"his father, and mother, and wife, and children, and brethren, and sisters, yea, and his own life also" (Luke 14:26). In other words, unless we have made him the supreme loyalty in our lives, we are not fully prepared to enter into the covenant. "Wherefore, *settle this in your hearts,* that ye will do the things which I shall teach, and command you" (JST Luke 14:28; emphasis added).

We may have made promises in the past and then failed to keep them, simply because afterward we didn't feel like doing what we said we would do. But if we will develop the capacity to make and keep promises, our sense of personal honor will gradually become much greater than our moods. And if we consistently keep our promises, everyone around us will eventually know that whatever we say will come to pass. We demonstrate honesty when our word conforms to reality, but we demonstrate *integrity* when reality conforms to our word—that is, when we create the reality. This gives us a sense of honor that empowers our relationships with the Lord and with other people.

Priesthood Power

Total and complete integrity is part of God's very nature. Because of his honor and the power and authority inherent in God's priesthood, the Lord can command the elements and all nature will respond. After all, was it not by this very power that he created the earth and the universe? During the Savior's mortal ministry, he was sleeping in a ship on the Sea of Galilee when "there arose a great storm of wind, and the waves beat into the ship. . . . And he arose, and rebuked the wind, and said unto the sea, Peace, be still. And the wind ceased, and there was a great calm" (Mark 4:37, 39). The Prophet Joseph Smith taught that this is one of the ways in which we can become like our Heavenly Father: "When a man works by faith he works by mental exertion instead of physical force. It is by words, instead of exerting his physical powers, with which every being works when he works by faith. God said, 'Let there be light: and there was light'" (*Lectures on Faith,* 7:3).

Jesus used this priesthood power throughout his ministry to perform many miracles, including healing the sick and afflicted and bringing the dead back to life. The apostles received power and authority from him to continue to bless and heal those who had faith and desire: "Is any sick among you? let him call for the elders of the church; and let them pray over him, anointing him with oil in the name of the Lord" (James 5:14). Healing by the laying on of hands is another example of how God's power is made manifest through the ordinances of the priesthood. Though it is evident that pain, sickness, and suffering are important and vital parts of our intentional growth and testing experience in mortality, and though healing is not always the highest blessing or will of the Father, the restoration of the priesthood in the latter days and its inherent power to bless and heal is a witness to God's perpetual love and concern for his children and his desire to honor those who exercise faith in him through *all* dispensations of time. A woman who had endured many years of surgeries and chemotherapy to combat cancer describes how the power of the priesthood worked in her own life to bless those who were treating her:

> The priesthood is a very important part of my life. In one of my blessings I was told that I would recover from the surgery and would be well for a season. Now, I don't know how long that season is going to be, but I know I have been blessed to have done as well as I have, and I cherish every day.
>
> When I first discovered the lump in my breast, I immediately made an appointment with a surgeon and for a mammogram. The lump was large and not difficult to detect. However, it did not show on the mammogram.

The surgeon said the protocol would be for me to return in three months and we would see if anything had changed. As I was scheduling my appointment with the receptionist, the doctor's nurse came to me and said that she and the doctor had just discussed my case, and that they had both felt impressed that they should treat my case more aggressively. Within a week I had a biopsy, which proved to be malignant, and a few days later I had a radical mastectomy.

Following eight months of chemotherapy, I was visiting with another doctor for a routine examination and she felt impressed to perform a test that revealed that I had colon cancer. During subsequent surgery to remove the cancer, the surgeon also found and removed a lesion on my liver that was malignant. Once again, a doctor was guided in my treatment.

The Second Birth

Almost from our infancy, we're saturated and immersed in the software of the world. That is why we must experience an equivalent immersion, even a greater immersion, through our covenant with Christ. This process of covenant-making releases the divine energy that enables us, under the influence of the Holy Ghost, to subordinate all of the programming of the first birth to the programming of the second birth.

The new birth consists of two parts: the baptism of water and the baptism of the Spirit. Each of these baptisms is an immersion that represents the death of the old person and the bringing forth of the new one. The baptism of water occurs very quickly, but the baptism of the Spirit takes time. President Spencer W. Kimball pointed out that Paul had to spend three years in the Arabian desert after his baptism in order to experience a spiritual rebirth: "Paul, the great apostle, could not seem to get into the spirit of his new calling until he had found cleansing solitude down in Arabia. He went into solitude a worldly man and came out cleansed, prepared, regenerated. He was born of water in a Damascus river and of the spirit in an Arabian solitude" (*Faith Precedes the Miracle*, 209).

We receive the Holy Ghost by covenant-making in the ordinances. Then we have a member of the Godhead who literally lives in us, and it's like the Father and the Son living in us. It gives us our new software and our new personality, and it eventually eclipses or subordinates all of the social programming and cultural software we have briefly picked up in our mortal experience.

In the words of one convert:

> When the gift of the Holy Ghost was bestowed upon me, it literally felt like going from the dark of night into the light for the first time. That was one thing I really prayed hard about: that Father in Heaven would help me feel the Spirit, help me to know that he was there. After the missionaries blessed me with the gift of the Holy Ghost, all the gospel principles became clear in my mind and easier to understand, whereas before it was like a fog.

"The Power of Godliness"

The ordinances of the priesthood have an effect on the human personality that cannot be achieved in any other way. The Lord has explained that the Melchizedek Priesthood "administereth the gospel and holdeth the key of the mysteries of the kingdom, even the key of the knowledge of God. Therefore, in the ordinances thereof, the power of godliness is manifest. And without the ordinances thereof, and the authority of the priesthood, the power of godliness is not manifest unto men in the flesh" (D&C 84:19–21).

What is this "power of godliness"? It is the power of perfection, the power to become like God. The key to this process is our *preparation* for the ordinances. We must be unified and repentant, we must have broken hearts and contrite spirits, so that we can enter into the gospel covenant and truly align ourselves with Christ. As we enter into a covenant relationship with him through priesthood ordinances, his power is transmitted into our being.

The Holy Ghost, as the attendant agent who seals and ratifies these ordinances, is sometimes called the "Holy Spirit of Promise." This expression is a reference to God's promise to his sons and daughters that, if we live true to our covenants, we will have "peace in this world, and eternal life in the world to come" (D&C 59:23). When we covenant with the Lord, he *also* covenants with us and slowly transfers his own nature into us by the power of the Holy Ghost. Satan has no power to match the powers of heaven, so he must stand aside and withdraw. The adversary cannot enter into our hearts as long as we remain deeply committed to the covenants we have made.

The Sacrament

The Lord has commanded us to *renew* our covenants and commitments every Sunday by partaking of the sacrament. This sacred time is a good opportunity for us to meditate upon *all* the covenants we have made.

When we eat an ordinary meal, we ask God to bless it to our bodies; but when we partake of the sacrament, we ask him to bless it to our souls—our eternal nature. We eat the bread and drink the water "in remembrance" of Jesus Christ. Perhaps one of the most important words in the scriptures is the word *remember.* When we remember the Lord and his goodness to us, all of the other fruits of the gospel are nourished within our souls. In the sacramental prayer, we also witness to our Father in Heaven that we are willing to keep his commandments. This is not a commitment to be perfect, but a commitment that we are *willing* to be obedient, that we will do the very best we can. And the Lord's promise is that if we honor our commitment, we "may always have his Spirit" to be with us.

I believe that sacrament meeting is the most significant hour of the entire week, because that hour will affect the quality of every other hour—if we approach it seriously and with deep commitment. In this world we are subject to the law of entropy, which dictates that everything falls apart and becomes disorganized. But through the sacrament, we may be constantly regenerated and renewed so that we keep improving and drawing nearer to God.

One woman tells how she learned to appreciate this sacred ordinance more fully:

> When I was pregnant with our last baby, I couldn't get to church for about the last three or four months, and the priests never came by to bring the sacrament to me. Finally, when I could go back to church, I insisted on being on time, getting there each week, and I remember when I insisted upon it, it became a priority to me. Then I could literally feel the power of the sacrament. It was overpowering. I finally realized there was much more to it than I had known before.

If the sacrament is only a habit or a social ritual to us, we may walk out of sacrament meeting and immediately begin to gossip about other people in a spirit of prejudice, cynicism, sarcasm, and cutting humor, because all of these things are the fruits of personal insecurity. But if the source of our security is Christ, and we constantly renew our covenant relationship with him, we will turn away from those things that are unworthy.

As with all ordinances, the key to the sacrament is to prepare ourselves in deep humility and sincerity and repentance, so that we are willing to fully commit our hearts to the Savior. When we do this, the power of the Atonement gives us a sense that our spiritual wounds are being healed, and the natural result is that we want to share that blessing with other people. We have no desire to judge or envy or gossip about them, because we are partaking of the powers of godliness, including the gift of charity.

Receiving the Holy Ghost

The first transcendent event of the Restoration relates primarily to God and man; it is "of the Father." The second event relates to Christ; it is "of the Son." And the third event relates to the Spirit; it is "of the Holy Ghost." Everyone who is confirmed a member of the Church is instructed to "receive the Holy Ghost." This means we are to take the initiative. We are given the gift of the Holy Ghost, but we must act in order to enjoy this gift. When we do so, we don't need to be in the presence of the Father and the Son. It's as if we're always with them, because the Holy Ghost is the revelator of their mind and will. He is also the testifier of their reality and their divinity—and of our own true nature. The Holy Ghost will purify and sanctify and make our personalities like that of Christ. He will also testify of Christ and bring us to him and comfort us. The Holy Ghost is manifested in the ordinances, and it took the priesthood or the power of God delegated to man to teach this gospel and administer these ordinances and then to set up the Church.

When we enter into the gospel covenant, we commit ourselves to a program of living by the commandments. There are basically two kinds of commandments: *general* commandments, which God gives to all people through the prophets, and *personal* commandments, which he gives to us individually through the Holy Ghost. And we don't receive the personal ones until we keep the general ones, because the Lord will not give us more light and knowledge if we fail to obey the light and knowledge he has already given. "For behold, thus saith the Lord God: I will give unto the children of men line upon line, precept upon precept, . . . for unto him that receiveth I will give more; and from them that shall say, We have enough, from them shall be taken away even that which they have" (2 Nephi 28:30). The Lord wants to bless and lift his children, not condemn them by giving them something before they are ready to receive it.

For instance, those who don't obey the Ten Commandments are usually not open to receiving the restored gospel. When people do accept the restored gospel, they are given additional general commandments such as tithing and the Word of Wisdom. And then they must obey these additional commandments in order to "receive the Holy Ghost" as an unending source of personal revelation. Those who do so will be "crowned with blessings from above, yea, and with commandments not a few, and with revelations in their time—they that are faithful and diligent before me" (D&C 59:4).

I am often asked by people for counsel and advice in their efforts to seek the will of God. I have learned to respond by saying, "In many matters, don't you already know his will?" They say, "Yes." I go on to ask, "Are you doing his will in those matters?" They usually say, "Well, not entirely." My response is, "Then don't seek his will; just do it. Then you'll find that personal commandments will come concerning his will on these other matters you are inquiring about."

The Guidance of the Holy Ghost

The Holy Ghost will give us very specific guidance if we will hear and act upon it. One woman tells of a personal commandment, or prompting, that she felt compelled to obey:

I was sitting in sacrament meeting with my family, and during the closing song, I noticed that a woman from the row next to us got up and left. The Spirit told me that I should call her. I tried to shrug off the feeling because I didn't even know her. We had exchanged hellos over the years, but I had never even really spoken with her. She was one of those women who seem to have everything together. I felt stupid about calling her, especially because I had no idea what to say.

When we got home from church, I had the feeling again that I should call. So I picked up the phone and called, having no idea what to say. Much to my relief, the line was busy. I thought to myself that I had done my part and that was that.

The next day I was painting my son's room when the feeling came again that I needed to call this woman. I tried ignoring it, but it just kept eating at me. So I stopped painting after a while and went to call. Again, much to my relief, the line was busy, and I felt like I was off the hook. I had tried calling twice, and that was good enough.

A couple of days later, I felt so strongly that I should call her that I decided to try one more time. This time her daughter answered and said that her mom wasn't home, but did I want to leave a message? How dumb would it be to leave my name when she didn't even know me at all? All I could think about was how this woman would wonder and think it strange that I called. But I left my name anyway, and told the daughter to have her mom give me a call when she had a chance. This time, as I hung up the phone, I said to myself that now I just had to be done. I had called twice, and then called again and left a message. I *had* to have done everything Heavenly Father wanted me to do!

The next Sunday in sacrament meeting, when I saw her walk in and sit down with her family, the Spirit hit me so hard, telling me that I should have called her and that I really needed to talk with her. So to get rid of this feeling I decided to talk with her after the meeting. Well, she was surrounded by friends and talking with a lot of people, and I felt a little silly walking up to her. She was so put together, and had so many friends; I didn't know what I would have to say that could be of any meaning to her.

But after some of the people dispersed I went up to her and said I wanted to talk to her. I pulled her to a corner of the chapel and just said, "All right, I just really need to get this off my chest. All week I have felt so prompted to call you and tell you that your Heavenly Father loves you." Tears came to her eyes, and she asked me when I was prompted to call her. I told her that when I saw her leave sacrament meeting last Sunday, I knew that I should call and tell her that Heavenly Father loved her. She said that those were the exact words she needed to hear. All week she had been struggling with self-doubt, and she desperately needed to hear those words, to know that Heavenly Father knew her, and that he loved her.

At that moment I realized that this was something I

needed to hear as well. Heavenly Father reminded me of who I was, that I was his child, and that he loved me.

If we're struggling with what to do with our lives, what decisions to make, we should determine whether we're keeping the commandments. If we're obeying the general commandments and are still struggling, we should ask ourselves whether we're keeping the Lord's personal commandments to us—the impressions of the Spirit by which we inwardly know the things we need to do.

The Effects of the Spirit

The apostle Paul said that when we receive the Spirit, it causes us to cry out, "Abba, Father" (Romans 8:15; Galatians 4:6). In other words, we have within us a deep internal spiritual memory that resonates to the Holy Ghost. And when we respond to the promptings he gives to us, we have an inward sense that our lives are being directed and conducted according to the Lord's will.

Once we receive the gift of the Holy Ghost, our internal software can expand dramatically. Not long ago I had the privilege of confirming my grandson Kameron a member of the Church. About a month later I was with him and his family while they were reading the Book of Mormon together. I was watching Kameron, and I noticed that he was marking the whole chapter we were reading. Afterward I asked him, "Why did you mark the whole chapter, Kameron?" His answer was, "Because it was such a good chapter." I also remember having a similar experience with my daughter Jenny soon after she was baptized.

I believe that we're influenced by the Holy Ghost during the first years of our childhood, but after we're baptized and confirmed we can have the permanent companionship of the Holy Ghost. The scriptures come alive to us, like living food and living water, and we can let our minds flow continuously over the words of eternal life so that our spirits are nourished by them. The Pearl of Great Price says that those who are born of the Spirit will "enjoy the words of eternal life" (Moses 6:59). That is the most fundamental exercise of all—the constant nourishment of our minds and spirits in the word of God. When we pull away from it, we find ourselves growing prideful, jealous, envious, and offended.

In order to enjoy the companionship of the Holy Ghost, we need to resist the numerous temptations of the world that would draw us away from the Spirit. I believe a person can resist and overcome temptation by creating a righteous response to temptation before it comes. This involves essentially going through a four-step mind-making-up process. *First,* feast on the words of Christ to cultivate a desire to know and do his will. *Second,* ask the Lord in deep prayer to give you a heightened awareness and sensitivity to temptation and tempting environments whenever they arise. *Third,* commit to the Lord that the moment he gives you such an awareness, you will immediately turn away and do some worthy thing—for example, inwardly singing a hymn, reviewing some memorized scriptures, or working on Church assignments. See yourself in your mind's eye confronting temptation and replacing it with good. *Fourth,* keep the commitment and gratefully report back.

Resisting Temptation: A Four-Step Process

| Keep the commitment and report back |

| Commit to replace temptation with good |

| Ask for heightened awareness |

| Feast on the words of Christ |

Feast on the Words of Christ

As we gain greater power over temptation, the Spirit abides with us continually. The Prophet Joseph Smith described what happens when a person actually receives the Holy Ghost: "A person may profit by noticing the first intimation of the spirit of revelation; for instance, when you feel pure intelligence flowing into you, it may give you sudden strokes of ideas, so that by noticing it, you may find it fulfilled the same day or soon; [that is,] those things that were presented unto your minds by the Spirit of God, will come to pass; and thus by learning the Spirit of God and understanding it, you may grow into the principle of revelation, until you become perfect in Christ Jesus" (*Teachings of the Prophet Joseph Smith,* 149–50, 151).

Again, fish discover water last. Many people cannot distinguish very much between their first birth and their second birth, simply because they grew up in an atmosphere in which they were constantly nurtured under the influence of the Holy Spirit and the teachings of the prophets. Thus when they are baptized and enter into the process of their second birth, the change isn't as noticeable to them as it is to people who haven't been brought up in that atmosphere.

I know I can never remember a time in my life when I did not feel a testimony of the truthfulness of the gospel. I used to wonder if I shouldn't have had more dramatic kinds of spiritual manifestations, especially when I heard and read about the experiences of some other people. But through my study I've come to believe that the second birth is sometimes a very natural process. I believe that as long as we feel confirmed in our minds and hearts regarding the gospel covenant, and as long as we follow the strait and narrow path—and keep coming back to it when we fail—we will, as Joseph Smith said, "grow into the principle of revelation" until we become perfect in Christ.

Partaking of the Divine Nature

When we are baptized into the Church, we are spiritually like infants rather than mature adults. The second birth is a process, not an instant transformation. Over a long period of time, we gradually become partakers of the divine nature under the tutelage and direction, the comfort, and the testifying influence of the Holy Ghost. One of the most beautiful and illuminating descriptions of this process that I have ever read was written by Elder Parley P. Pratt:

> An intelligent being, in the image of God, possesses every organ, attribute, sense, sympathy, [and] affection that is possessed by God himself.
>
> But these are possessed by man, in his rudimental state, in a subordinate sense of the word. Or, in other words, these attributes are in embryo and are to be gradually developed. They resemble a bud, a germ, which gradually develops into bloom, and then, by progress, produces the mature fruit after its own kind.
>
> The gift of the Holy Ghost adapts itself to all these organs or attributes. It quickens all the intellectual faculties, increases, enlarges, expands, and purifies all the natural passions and affections, and adapts them, by the gift of wisdom, to their lawful use. It inspires, develops, cultivates, and matures all the fine-toned sympathies, joys, tastes, kindred feelings, and affections of our nature. It inspires virtue, kindness, goodness, tenderness, gentleness, and charity. It develops beauty of person, form, and features. It tends to health, vigor, animation, and social

feeling. It invigorates all the faculties of the physical and intellectual man. It strengthens and gives tone to the nerves. In short, it is, as it were, marrow to the bone, joy to the heart, light to the eyes, music to the ears, and life to the whole being. . . . Such is the gift of the Holy Ghost, and such are its operations when received through the lawful channel—the divine, eternal priesthood (*Key to the Science of Theology,* 61–62).

President James E. Faust has described how the Holy Ghost can help cultivate the divine potential within each person:

> The Holy Ghost bears witness of the truth and impresses upon the soul the reality of God the Father and the Son Jesus Christ so deeply that no earthly power or authority can separate [a person] from that knowledge. . . .
>
> I believe the Spirit of the Holy Ghost is the greatest guarantor of inward peace in our unstable world. It can be more mind-expanding and can make us have a better sense of well-being than any chemical or other earthly substance. It will calm nerves; it will breathe peace to our souls. This Comforter can be with us as we seek to improve. It can function as a source of revelation to warn us of impending danger and also help keep us from making mistakes. It can enhance our natural senses so that we can see more clearly, hear more keenly, and remember what we should remember. It is a way of maximizing our happiness. . . .
>
> The Spirit—the Holy Ghost—will help us work out our insecurities. For instance, it can help us learn to forgive. . . .
>
> In simple terms, the gift of the Holy Ghost is

an enhanced spiritual power permitting those entitled thereto . . . to receive a greater knowledge and enjoyment of the influence of Deity. . . .

I testify that as we mature spiritually under the guidance of the Holy Ghost, our sense of personal worth, of belonging, and of identity increases. . . . I would rather have every person enjoy the Spirit of the Holy Ghost than any other association, for they will be led by that Spirit to light and truth and pure intelligence, which can carry them back into the presence of God ("The Gift of the Holy Ghost: A Sure Compass," *Ensign,* April 1996, 4–6).

Internalizing the Third Event

At a large missionary conference, someone once asked President Harold B. Lee, "What is the most important commandment?" President Lee looked at the missionary for a long time, perhaps discerning his spirit, and then said, "Elder, the most important commandment is the one you are having the greatest difficulty living."

Many times over the years, I've asked people to ponder in their hearts the answers to these questions: "What is the commandment you have the greatest difficulty with? What do you need to do to draw closer to the Lord? What do you need to do to be a better husband and father, a better wife and mother, or a better member of the Church?" As they have thought about these questions, I've asked them to listen to the impressions of the Spirit and to write those impressions on paper. The Holy Ghost can bring to our remembrance all things that Christ has taught us (see John 14:26). When we ponder about our decisions in life, these truths come into our consciousness so that they can be written down.

The Savior said that the Holy Ghost will guide us into all truth and will even show us things to come (see John 16:13). But in order to receive these personal revelations, we must keep the commandments we have already been given. So the personal initiative for this event is to obey the commandments, as we covenant to do when we are baptized—a covenant we renew each week as we partake of the sacrament. Then, we can take what we learn to a more advanced level and follow the "personal commandments" we are given through the Spirit, strengthening and rebuilding relationships through forgiveness and love as we are strengthened by the Savior's forgiveness and love in the covenants that we make with him.

Basic Level— Personal Initiatives	Advanced Level— Enlarging Service Initiatives
1. Offer daily, listening prayers of faith.	1. Build strong human relationships through profound listening, affirming, and caring service.
2. Ponder the scriptures daily to feast on the words and love of Jesus Christ. ("Give us this day our daily bread.")	2. Teach and testify, by the Spirit, of Christ and his atoning sacrifice.
3. Exercise "repentance unto baptism," or partake of the sacrament worthily (obeying "general commandments"—becoming perfect *in* Christ).	3. Forgive all others and rebuild wounded relationships, as guided by the Spirit (obeying "personal commandments").

THE RESTORATION
OF THE CHURCH

WHERE DO I GO TO RECEIVE CHRIST?

CHAPTER 7

THE FOURTH EVENT: THE RESTORATION OF THE CHURCH

WHERE DO I GO TO RECEIVE CHRIST?

S OON AFTER RECEIVING THE PRIESTHOOD, Joseph Smith and Oliver Cowdery "engaged in solemn and fervent prayer" to seek further direction. As a result, the Lord gave them a series of revelations indicating what he wanted them to do. Joseph said that one of these revelations "pointed out to us the precise day upon which . . . we should proceed to organize His Church once more here upon the earth" (*History of the Church,* 1:60, 64). In accordance with this commandment, The Church of Jesus Christ of Latter-day Saints was established on April 6, 1830. This crucial event brought into being the kingdom of God, foretold by the ancient prophet Daniel, which will eventually fill the whole earth (see Daniel 2:28–44).

In my professional work with organizations, both private and public, I have observed the absolute need to formalize a structure that embodies the organization's principles, purposes, mission, values, and vision—in other words, the big ideas behind the whole enterprise. These literally have to be built right into the structure, systems, and processes of the organization, or there will be no lasting legacy in that organization. When new leaders come in, everything can change, and if those leaders are bad ones, the organization will probably die. This process of building principles into structures, systems, and processes that enable such continuity is called "institutionalizing." Thus the Constitution of the United States institutionalized the principles of the Declaration of Independence, which has enabled the United States to survive major traumas to its national life, including the Civil War, the Vietnam War, impeachments, scandals, and other crises.

It was imperative that a church be established to *institutionalize* the previous three events of the Restoration—the eternal principles and purposes and powers that had been restored. This eliminated the dependency upon particular leaders or a particular controlling group. It also minimized the effects of adverse external forces or internal traumas, which otherwise could have been catastrophic.

One of the most significant evidences of the truth and strength of the Church is how it has transcended the major traumas it has experienced from the beginning. In fact, this would apply as much to mature stakes and wards as it does to the entire Church. Just notice what happens when a new stake presidency or bishopric is installed and is sustained by the people and ordained by priesthood leaders. There is almost always an increased sense of unity, a higher level of devotion and dedication and spirituality, even though sometimes relatively unknown people have been installed as the new leaders. This stands in dramatic contrast to what almost always happens with worldly organizations that change leaders—there is often a big political game, and many people are upset and traumatized and become disaffected and polarized. You particularly see this when mergers take place between organizations that have different cultural underpinnings. It is an amazing thing to watch the change of leadership in stakes and wards, as well as in the Church as a whole, and to contrast it with the secular organizations that all of us belong to in the world.

When the Church was established formally, it essentially *institutionalized the gospel,* which made gospel principles sustainable over time and circumstance. Institutionalizing the Savior's purpose into an organization that mirrors his divine mission creates opportunities to live as the Savior lived. Within the Church organization, we can make and keep the sacred covenants of baptism, the sacrament, and temple endowments and marriage, offering up our will to the Father, offering up our lives in sacrificial service for the benefit of our fellow beings. If we follow these principles, roles, patterns, and opportunities with exactness, we can, with the aid of the Spirit, experience the abundant life in Christ.

This is not accomplished without difficulty. All who come to the gospel and the Church must wean themselves from the world's comparison culture and graft themselves to the root of the Lord's vine: the abundance of the gospel, the eternal blessings that will flow to us from the goodness of God and our own obedience to his commandments (see John 15:1–12). This requires us to lay down on the altar our weaknesses, our lack of faith, our envy and jealousies—which sometimes make life so interesting for us—and our comparison-based sense of self-worth, which makes us feel falsely important. Then we must be willing to let the Lord polish us like a stone with the demands of membership in his Church and kingdom.

Some people resist organized religion. They say it stifles the human spirit, robbing the individual of agency and the ability to make choices. They're operating out of a scarcity mind-set that views the interdependence needed to be a part of the body of Christ as being limiting or restrictive. In reality, activity in the gospel and in the attendant Church programs, with their endless opportunities for growth and development, is magnificently liberating and expansive and can only lead one toward all that the Father hath.

Always remember that at the heart of the Church organization flows the lifeblood of the Atonement, the saving principles and ordinances of the gospel as administered through Christ's ordained servants on the earth. Hence the restoration of the Church answers the question "Where do we go to receive the ordinances and covenants of Christ's gospel?" I suggest that the Church also provides three other important things: a support system for its members, order and direction to take the gospel to all people, on both sides of the veil, and opportunities for the Saints to grow and develop toward perfection.

A Support System

The Book of Mormon describes the nurturing that was given to those who joined the Lord's church in ancient America: "After they had been received unto baptism, and were wrought upon and cleansed by the power of the Holy Ghost, they were numbered among the people of the church of Christ; and their names were taken, that they might be remembered and nourished by the good word of God, to keep them in the right way, to keep them continually watchful unto prayer, relying alone upon the merits of Christ, who was the author and the finisher of their faith" (Moroni 6:4).

The Church follows the same pattern today, because all

people need a support system. If we examine the significant organizations and programs that societies have created to help people improve their lives, we find that they always involve some kind of support system to provide encouragement and affirmation. We are all human beings with hearts that need to be loved and nourished and cultivated. And those who have entered into the gospel covenant need to feel Christ's love, not only through his Spirit but also through other people who share their commitment to the Savior. When they experience this love, it has a tendency to "keep them in the right way," the path of eternal life.

As I've studied the total program of the Church, I've come to realize that it serves every need of man's nature—not only his spiritual needs but in part his physical, educational, and social needs as well. This realization has strengthened my testimony that the Church is truly God's kingdom on earth. It is a magnificent organization; there is no institution anywhere to compare with it. It lifts anyone who gets involved with it to a much higher level. It is a church of works, service, and contribution based on faith in Jesus Christ. It deals not only with man's earthly condition but also with the processes that deeply change a human soul, because its ultimate object is the salvation, perfection, and exaltation of God's children.

Order and Direction to Accomplish the Lord's Work

Another reason for the Church organization is to provide an orderly way to take the first three events of the Restoration—a correct knowledge of God and of ourselves, a true understanding of Christ and his atonement, and an opportunity to enter into the gospel covenant through the ordinances of the priesthood—to all people on both sides of the veil. Our Heavenly Father has commanded that the gospel and its ordinances be made available to everyone, both the living and the dead, because he loves all of his children.

Of course, there must be some kind of directing authority and coordination to see that this work is done properly and effectively. "Behold, mine house is a house of order, saith the Lord God, and not a house of confusion" (D&C 132:8). Thus, under priesthood authority, the necessary structures and systems have been established to proclaim the gospel, perfect the Saints, and redeem the dead.

The Lord relies on his covenant people to accomplish these things. When we receive the Atonement through our obedience to the laws and ordinances of the gospel, we're paid for. Our lives have been bought by the suffering of our Savior, and we become his stewards. And what do stewards do? They take his gospel to the rest of the world. Thus we are to "stand as witnesses of God at all times . . . and in all places" (Mosiah 18:9).

Personal Growth and Development

I suggest that the third reason for the Church is to provide constant opportunities for our own growth and development. We need these opportunities in order to move toward perfection, because being born again through baptism is only the beginning. We're just new infants. But when we become active and involved in the Church, we have an organized way to continue the expansion of our celestial software.

Some of this growth comes through attending meetings, where we partake of the sacrament and receive gospel instruction—and thus get feedback that helps us return to the strait and narrow path. But much of the growth we experience in the Church is the result of profound testing. The Church provides the most powerful support system in the world, but at the same time it exposes us to challenge and risk. For example, we're often called to serve other people, and this process requires us to be open and vulnerable. We don't know what's going to happen, and we're asked to do all kinds of things.

One woman tells what she learned about herself through accepting callings that stretched her capacity:

> Any calling you receive will stretch and strengthen you. The details of my calling may be different from the details of your calling, but all callings performed for the Lord in the name of the Lord should bring you to the Lord. This is what my calling has done for me. As I have gone out to serve the sisters, I have prayed to know what exactly is my mission for the Lord. When I serve, I try to be a worthy representative of him in all that I say and do. I always fall short, but he is quick to forgive.
>
> I have learned that I am more than I thought I was. Before my calling I had a testimony, but I never would have thought it could be tremendously useful for others outside of my own family. In fact, I was very timid in sharing my testimony even with my family. Now that the Lord is requiring a greater commitment of service from me outside of my home, I have come to understand that my testimony can really strengthen others. When I bear my testimony to a sister in the ward, I'm surprised at the words that come out of my mouth. I'll catch myself thinking, "Did that just come from me?" If I bear my testimony after sharing a lesson, I'm shocked if my words sounded greater than just babbling. By bearing my testimony frequently through the opportunities my calling affords me, I gain confidence that my life really has

meaning and that I can in fact make a difference in the lives of those I serve.

We may be called to do things that we think are beyond our capacity, and this humbles us to such an extent that we have to rely on God to make us equal to the challenge. In some cases we may receive callings that we enjoy, and as soon as we get comfortable we're called into an entirely different kind of activity. It may even be something that we initially don't want to do, because it doesn't seem to be congruent with our own talents and interests and dispositions.

Another cultural tendency is to become lawless, or a law unto ourselves; we believe, expect, or suggest that *we* should choose what we do in the ward and stake. Yet another is to simply submit to ward and stake leaders and do whatever we are called to do, regardless of our circumstances. We often tend to ignore the third alternative of sharing information about our circumstances and then submitting to the informed and inspired decisions of our leaders.

Sometimes we're called to serve in "higher" positions, and afterward we're released and called to serve in "lower" positions. For some people, accepting a release may be even more difficult than accepting a call. But these changes give us an opportunity to learn the principle taught by President J. Reuben Clark, Jr.: "In the service of the Lord, it is not where you serve but how" (Conference Report, April 1951, 154).

Every time we are given a calling, we should gratefully and graciously be aware that a time will come when we will be released from that calling. Then when that time does come, we are both grateful and gracious.

After serving as a regional representative for many years, my brother John was called as Young Men's president in his ward, which tested him in entirely new ways. I also served as a regional representative and as a member of several general Church boards and committees, and then I was called as a Primary teacher. My son and about four other children were in the class. They didn't listen to me, and I was a little uncomfortable in that calling. My son said, "Dad, they think you're a nerd." So I had to seek his advice about what I could do to make the class more interesting.

Thus we're alternately humbled by the challenges of the different callings we receive. These are all part of the testing and refining we experience through our service in the Church. The Lord uses this process to throw us out of our comfort zones so that he can develop many parts of our nature and smooth out the rough places in our character.

Our callings in the Church also place us in a world of interdependence, a world in which we have to deal with many individuals and leaders who think, feel, and act differently than we do. Since all of them are far from perfect, many things will happen that may be misunderstood or even offensive.

If we're not centered in Christ and his gospel, we can be disturbed and uprooted by the changes and human problems that are part of our experience in the Church. Some members become so deeply focused on these things that they are almost consumed by them. But an essential aspect of the Church's strength is that it's a lay church, not a professional organization, which provides opportunities for everyone to grow. Even our young people, from the time they're little Primary children, are invited to speak in meetings and participate in other ways until they're prepared to serve missions and eventually to receive the eternal blessings of the temple.

We may sometimes wish we could avoid this vulnerable state in which we have to deal with people who have so many weaknesses and are so different from us. It may seem that it would be a lot safer to stay in a cloistered environment and focus on our personal relationship with the Lord, clothed in the feeling of his acceptance and salvation. But when we're baptized into his church, we enter into a covenant to serve him until the end of our lives (see Mosiah 18:13; Moroni 6:3; D&C 20:37)—and that means serving our fellowmen.

It's only through gospel service that we internalize Christ's teachings so that they can become part of our nature. We learn love and patience only on the gristmill of experience; they can't be grown in a vacuum. Furthermore, true service—the "second mile" kind of service—is usually inconvenient. It involves sacrifice, self-denial, and the subordination of our own desires to a higher purpose. To serve in this way, we can't be motivated by a "should" spirit or a duty spirit; we must act out of true feelings of love. And it's through our service in God's kingdom that he gradually sanctifies and perfects our souls.

Consider this woman's testimony of the power of serving with love:

> One day I was sitting at a table in my kitchen, and I had this feeling that this sister in our ward needed to know that the Lord loved her. It was kind of a weird thing—I thought, *She needs a fruit basket.* So I ran out to the store, spent half a fortune, came back, made this grand and glorious fruit basket with cellophane and the whole thing, and I was sitting there looking at it thinking, *You idiot.* I was just staring at this fruit basket, and by now it was noon, and she called on the phone. She was crying and saying, "Nobody loves me; nobody knows I exist."
>
> And I said, "Your Heavenly Father knows you exist. Answer the door." She was only two minutes away, so I got in my car and went over there and handed her the fruit basket. I had a note to her and the whole thing, so

she knew I couldn't have thrown that together in those two minutes between my house and her house. I said, "Heavenly Father knows."

That was just a feeling, but I'm so glad that I acted upon those feelings. I think that when we have the feelings and act upon them, that's how our testimony grows.

Receiving by Giving

I have received witnesses of the Spirit primarily as I have taught others the gospel, bearing testimony to people of the Restoration and the truthfulness of it. It is like strengthening a muscle—only in its use do we develop it so we can use it more fully. We knew of the gospel in the premortal life, but it is obscured from our consciousness in mortality until we teach and testify about it and pray for it; then the testimony develops. I can honestly say that my greatest learning and insights have come from teaching in order to reach people, different kinds of people, people from different cultures with different frames of reference. The very effort to adapt and be flexible to accommodate their realities causes me to learn and to grow and to extend myself through other dimensions of my personality.

Centered in Christ, Not in the Church

I received the following letter from a woman who was baptized more than thirty years ago:

I converted to the Church at the age of eighteen. I later married in the temple and had seven children. Over the years I served as a teacher and an officer in several auxiliaries on the ward and stake levels. The Church gave a pattern to my life, and I felt complete.

In 1980 the Church introduced the block meeting schedule, and I've never been able to adjust to this radical change in what had been a very comforting pattern. We used to have Relief Society on Tuesday, Primary on Wednesday, MIA on Thursday, and so forth. Since the change, I just can't seem to bond with anybody when we move into a new ward. I used to be able to get to know the sisters at Relief Society, but now I feel very lonely and also very bitter—these feelings feed off of each other. I feel as if the Lord has tricked me and led me into a trap, the bait being a way of life that once offered me security. I feel abandoned, and I'm growing increasingly bitter. Apostate groups are beginning to offer an outlet for my pent-up rage.

Intellectually, I know I'm wrong. I long for the feelings I once had, but when I attend church I feel that I'm only rubbing my nose in the source of my problem. . . . I would *love* to get back to wherever I jumped the tracks and end this dance of death. I desperately want to solve this problem.

I appreciate this woman's honesty, and I believe that many Latter-day Saints can identify with the struggle she is having. Every change that is made in the Church affects people's lives in different ways. The General Authorities introduced the consolidated meeting schedule to reduce the travel requirements that were burdening the Saints in many areas and to allow more time for the family in today's fast-paced world. But this change has also produced other consequences, and we may need to find ways to compensate for them.

The key is to get back to the first three events in the Lord's model. We must regain a sense of our true identity and our relationship with Heavenly Father through sincere and earnest prayer. We must strengthen our relationship with Christ and our understanding of his gospel by studying the scriptures and deeply pondering the Atonement. And we must recommit ourselves to the covenants we have entered into so that we can enjoy the guidance and gifts of the Spirit.

If the woman who wrote that letter will take the initiative to personally experience these three events every day, the Holy Ghost will help her adjust socially and emotionally to the block meeting schedule. He will fully compensate for what she has lost and will eventually help her build friendships with other members of her ward, even though it may be difficult. For a time she may have to get her fellowshipping from her Heavenly Father and his Spirit, but in response to her earnest prayers and her own efforts, the Lord can also cause people to cross her path who will bring her the human nurturing she needs.

We must build our lives, not on the Church, but rather on Christ and his gospel. When we do that, we are able to contribute to the Church and help it become more and more like Christ and his gospel. He said, "It is my church, if it so be that they [the members] are built upon my gospel. . . . And if it so be that the church is built upon my gospel then will the Father show forth his own works in it" (3 Nephi 27:8, 10).

The Shepherd, the Sheepherder, and the Sheep— Three Models of Leadership

As we build our lives on Christ, we serve his children as he would. Christ referred to himself as "the good shepherd [who] giveth his life for the sheep" (John 10:11). Peter called him "the Shepherd and Bishop of your souls . . . [who] suffered for us, leaving us an example, that [we] should follow his steps" (1 Peter 2:25, 21).

Good leaders are *shepherds,* and their people are their sheep. The shepherds know their sheep. They know their sheep's voices, for they know their aspirations and fears, their worries and doubts, their families and their problems. Shepherds have genuinely listened to their sheep. Shepherds care for their sheep; they care very sincerely. They appreciate their sheep. They love their sheep so much that they would lay down their lives for their sheep if they had to. Shepherds show their love in innumerable ways— little acts of kindness, patience, forbearance, understanding, and compassion. They'll go the second mile for their sheep. When one of the sheep strays, the shepherd leaves the ninety-nine and lovingly brings it back into the fold. This spirit of valuing the one lost sheep is the same spirit that keeps the other ninety-nine in the fold.

Sheep also know their shepherd. They have heard the shepherd's voice. Shepherds do not pretend to be someone they are not. Shepherds are no "tin gods" who stand apart and are difficult to approach or talk with. Rather, shepherds lead their sheep. They do not need to drive the sheep, because the sheep know their shepherds' voice and will follow it, and therefore the shepherd can go before them, leading them from the front.

On the other hand, *sheepherders* have to drive their sheep. They have to push and cajole and beg and hover in order to get things done. They have to drive because they do not know their sheep, and the sheep do not know their sheepherders. Such leaders have never really listened to their sheep and don't really care for them; they care instead for their wages. A sheepherder is a hired hand, working from a "what's in it for me" viewpoint. The wages may be glory or honor, or the power and control a position bestows. Sheepherders may even aspire to a higher position or one of greater social honor. Because of their double-mindedness, their voices ring hollow and are the voices of strangers. Such officers or teachers do not need to wonder why attendance in their wards is low, why the activities lack "punch." If they're honest, they'll examine their own hearts and study the roots of the instability.

When things don't go well, or when sheepherders are criticized (approaches of the wolf), these hired hands leave their sheep. "The hireling fleeth, because he is an hireling, and careth not for the sheep" (John 10:13). They leave by giving excuses, by asking for other jobs, by indifference and complacency, or by becoming sheep themselves.

Then there are the *sheep* who merely "go along," and as sheep leaders and teachers, they may do just what they have to do in order to "get by"—no real drive or enthusiasm or fire anymore! Everything becomes dead-level mediocrity. Rather than acting upon this unhappy situation and striving to radiate a new spirit, these sheep absorb the existing spirit. They're imitators, not creators. They're victims, not masters. They're sheep, not shepherds.

The most important factor in leadership is this: How much do you really care for your people? And how noble and important is the purpose? How much do you feel this deep inside, this sincere caring for each of the individuals in your Sunday School class, in the Scout troop, in the office, or at home? Leaders are often tossed and turned by every wind of new leadership doctrine (see Ephesians 4:14). Should they be more democratic or more autocratic in action? Firmer or more permissive?

Those questions are important and must be considered, but they are secondary questions. The primary question is, Do you really care? If you answer that question affirmatively, you can make some mistakes on the other questions and still be successful. But if you answer it negatively, you may have all the right answers to the other questions, but you cannot succeed.

Shepherds, Sheepherders, and Sheep

	SHEPHERD	HIRED SHEEPHERDER	SHEEP
Motive	Love of sheep	Love of wage	Safety, belonging
Communication	Honest ("for they know his voice," John 10:4) Two-way ("and am known of mine," John 10:14)	Dishonest, disguised ("know not the voice of strangers," John 10:5)	Self-concerned, one-way
Leadership	Leads in front by example through love	Drives from behind, or carrot-and-stick approach	Follows—no vision—just goes along
Consequences	Safety—salvation, self-realization, eternal life	Sheep deserted in stormy times (when wolf approaches), leaderless and scattered	Course of least resistance

To become a shepherd, follow the true Shepherd (see John 10:1–15). The accompanying chart summarizes some of the differences between shepherds, sheepherders, and sheep.

Helping the Saints Reach a Higher Level

Whenever we have an opportunity to call or recommend others to serve in the Church, we should look for ways to draw out their inner strengths. One way to do that is to treat them in terms of their celestial potential rather than in terms of their present attitudes and behavior. The German writer Goethe said, "Treat a man as he is and he will remain as he is; treat a man as he can and should be and he will become as he can and should be."

By involving people in serving the Lord, we help them become their best and highest selves. President Thomas S. Monson told a story that demonstrates this kind of growth resulting from service:

> I recall that as a bishop, one morning the boys in the ward over which I presided had assembled—sleepy-eyed, a bit disheveled, and mildly complaining about arising so early to fulfill their assignment. Not a word of reproof was spoken, but during the following week we escorted the boys to Welfare Square in Salt Lake City for a guided tour. They saw firsthand a lame sister operating the telephone switchboard, an older man stocking shelves, women arranging clothing to be distributed—even a blind person placing labels on cans of food. Here were individuals earning their sustenance through their contributed labors. A penetrating silence came over the boys as they witnessed how their effort each month helped to collect the sacred fast offering funds which aided the needy and provided employment for those who otherwise would be idle.
>
> From that hallowed day forward, we no longer had to urge our deacons with regard to collecting fast offerings. On fast Sunday mornings, they were present at 7:00 A.M., dressed in their Sunday best, anxious to do their duty as holders of the Aaronic Priesthood. No longer were they simply distributing and collecting envelopes. They were helping to provide food for the hungry and shelter for the homeless—all after the way of the Lord ("Be Thou an Example," *Ensign,* November 1996, 44).

The Family: The True MTC

President Gordon B. Hinckley has challenged the Church to raise the bar so that missionaries are more qualified, more worthy, more committed, and more spiritually minded. This increased effort and preparation will enable them to truly teach by the Spirit instead of primarily following scripts. This puts a greater responsibility on families, which are the *true* Missionary Training Centers. This puts a greater responsibility on priesthood leaders to empower parents and individuals and young people more and more with the responsibility to exercise their own initiative in accomplishing God's purposes. As the scriptures counsel us, "Men should be anxiously engaged in a good cause, and do many things of their own free will, and bring to pass much righteousness" (D&C 58:27).

Taking Initiative

In the Worldwide Leadership Training Session conducted in January 2004, Elder Richard G. Scott taught:

There is an irrigation analogy normally used in the Church of "getting the water to the end of the row." However, at stake and ward levels, it would be far better for you priesthood leaders and auxiliary officers to simply "let it rain" from heaven. Your sacred callings give you the divine right to inspiration. Confidently seek it. Wherever you live in the world, in the smallest branch or the largest ward, a struggling district or a fully organized stake, you have the right to be guided in fulfilling your inspired assignment to best meet the needs of those you serve.

This powerful counsel suggests that all of us need to exercise our own *initiative* more often within the bounds of our stewardships. The idea is this: *That which is not prohibited is allowed.* This gives a whole different sense and feeling of empowerment than its opposite—that which is not expressly permitted is implicitly prohibited. Think what could happen in home teaching, visiting teaching, parenting, and missionary work if members were empowered to really use the gifts of the Holy Spirit within the framework of gospel principles. We would move beyond merely fulfilling Church callings to magnifying the calls to service we receive through the Spirit.

Inviting Others Back into the Fold through Callings

Everyone has a contribution to make, if we can only help them see it and empower them to act upon what they feel. Those who have withdrawn from the Church may initially resist our efforts, but we can reassure them about their capabilities and affirm our personal belief in them. Callings must be extended under the inspiration of the Spirit, of course, by those who are in a position to receive such inspiration. And these leaders have a tremendous stewardship to reach out to others and essentially say to them, "You are to be a contributor. You're a part of this kingdom, so rather than just sit by and criticize and expect to be nurtured continuously, you are to help make this a better ward, a better branch, a better quorum, a better auxiliary. You can make a great difference. Get back into the harvest and contribute."

A woman describes the opportunity she was given to grow and repent through accepting a calling:

I think the most important thing to ever happen to me was when I was given a calling. The bishop called me in to give me a calling, not knowing that I couldn't accept the calling until I had repented of some things. What was supposed to be a five-minute thing turned into an hour-and-a-half interview of clearing up my life, but it was the best thing that I ever did. I was able to start clean, and then he extended the calling to me, which was unbelievable.

I started in with the Merrie Miss girls in Primary, where I was able to achieve the growth I had never made. Everything I taught those girls was something I needed to experience myself. I spent two years with the same girls in the Merrie Miss program and then moved into the Young Women program. I was able to read and study and give those lessons, and they were everything that I had never received. And I just flourished.

Those who respond to such inspired calls are affected in powerful ways. As they get a vision of Zion and begin to help build the kingdom of God, an amazing thing happens to them. This is illustrated beautifully in the following story told by Elder Jeffrey R. Holland:

> The Brethren used to announce at general conference the names of those who had been called on missions. Not only was this the way friends and neighbors learned of the call, but more often than not it was the way the missionary learned of it as well. One such prospect was Eli H. Pierce. A railroad man by trade, he had not been very faithful in the Church. . . . His mind had been given totally to what he demurely called "temporalities." He said he had never read more than a few pages of scripture in his life, that he had spoken at only one public gathering (an effort that he says "was no credit" to himself or those who heard him), and he used the vernacular of the railroad and barroom with a finesse born of long practice. He bought cigars wholesale—a thousand at a time—and he regularly lost his paycheck playing pool. . . .

Well, the Lord knew what Eli Pierce was and he knew something else. He knew what Eli Pierce could become. When the call came that October 5, 1875, Eli wasn't even in the Tabernacle. He was out working on one of the railroad lines. A fellow employee, once he had recovered from the shock of it all, ran out to telegraph the startling news. Brother Pierce writes: "At the very moment this intelligence was being flashed over the wires, I was sitting lazily thrown back in an office rocking chair, my feet on the desk, reading a novel and simultaneously sucking on an old Dutch pipe just to vary the monotony of cigar smoking. As soon as I had been informed of what had taken place, I threw the novel in the wastebasket, the pipe in the corner (and have never touched either to this hour). I sent in my resignation . . . to take effect at once, in order that I might have time for study and preparation. I then started into town to buy [scripture]."

Then Eli wrote these stirring words: "Remarkable as it may seem, and has since appeared to me, a thought of disregarding the call, or of refusing to comply with the requirement, never once entered my mind. The only question I asked—and I asked it a thousand times—was: How can I accomplish this mission? How can I, who am so shamefully ignorant and untaught in doctrine, do honor to God and justice to the souls of men, and merit the trust reposed in me by the Priesthood?"

With such genuine humility fostering resolution rather than defeating it, Eli Pierce fulfilled a remarkable mission. His journal could appropriately close on a completely renovated life with this one line: "Throughout our entire mission we were greatly blessed." But I add one experience to make the point.

During the course of his missionary service, Brother Pierce was called in to administer to the infant child of a branch president whom he knew and loved. Unfortunately the wife of the branch president had become embittered and now seriously objected to any religious activity within the home, including a blessing for this dying child. With the mother refusing to leave the bedside and the child too ill to move, the humble branch president with his missionary friend Eli retired to a small upper room in the house to pray for the baby's life. The mother, suspecting just such an act, sent one of the older children to observe and report back.

There in that secluded chamber the two men knelt and prayed fervently until, in Brother Pierce's own words, "we felt that the child would live and knew that our prayers had been heard." Arising from their knees, they turned slowly only to see the young girl standing in the partially open doorway gazing intently into the room. She seemed, however, quite oblivious to the movements of the two men. She stood entranced for some seconds, her eyes immovable. Then she said, "Papa, who was that man in there?" Her father said, "That is Brother Pierce. You know him." "No," she said matter-of-factly, "I mean the *other* man." "There was no other, darling, except Brother Pierce and myself. We were praying for the baby." "Oh, there was another man," the child insisted, "for I saw him standing [above] you and Brother Pierce and he was dressed in white." Now if God in his heavens will do that for a repentant old cigar-smoking, inactive, stern-swearing pool player, don't you think he'll do it for you? He will if your resolve is as deep and permanent as Eli Pierce's. In the Church we ask for faith, not infallibility. (*However Long and Hard the Road,* 7–9.)

The Lord is watching us, and he uses his church as an instrument to hone us, develop us, and perfect us. He has given us special gifts in mortality, and if we exercise and magnify those gifts, he will give us more and more. If we're willing to do things outside our comfort zones, opening ourselves to new experiences, we learn new dimensions of our nature. We learn that we have enormous capacity. Ultimately we will learn that we may develop the capacity of God the Eternal Father, because we are literally his children.

Internalizing the Fourth Event

Becoming involved in the great organization of the Church offers numerous opportunities to grow, progress, and regularly experience all the events of the Restoration. The personal initiative for this chapter invites us to keep our covenants more fully by *magnifying the callings* we receive through formal, priesthood channels.

But we can also build the kingdom by magnifying our "personal callings," those we feel prompted by the Spirit to carry out, as the service initiative suggests. Those who strive to be like Christ see all of life as a mission in the Lord's cause—as a *stewardship.* Divine, nurturing sources have armed and prepared them for his service, to do his work with his other children. A major challenge of life is that of service. We halt the necessary growth process by achieving a certain level of righteousness in keeping the general commandments and leaving it at that. Because our culture would sufficiently reward us for faithfulness in such a circumstance, we might be tempted not to continue educating our consciences to receive personal commandments regarding opportunities to serve. These may be outside the "job definitions" of our present duties within the family, the Church, or the world.

I remember a defining moment in my own church and professional work years ago in a personal priesthood interview I attended with one of the apostles in my role as a regional representative. In one of the stakes I was assigned to, only around 20 percent of the young men were serving missions and marrying in the temple. The apostle was very familiar with the stake and with the town, which had an LDS population of about 50 percent. He asked what I was doing to get more young people on missions and into the temple. I responded that I was acutely aware of the problem and was working with the priesthood leaders to strengthen the effort and the Church programs to keep the young men faithful and desirous of serving missions, but also that the "cool thing," the social norm, was not to go. I was at a loss to think of anything else except to try harder.

The apostle challenged me to "think outside the box." He knew that most of the community and social leaders were members of other faiths, that the town culture was quite worldly, and also that the strong leaders were extremely busy doing "Church work" in bishoprics, high councils, and other leadership positions. He suggested that I consider encouraging the callings of some of these faithful "old-timers" to encompass community service jobs, including running for political office, serving on school boards, and joining social clubs. In turn, we might call younger faithful brethren, to whom the young men could relate more easily, to positions of Church leadership. In this way, we could influence the social mores and norms of both community and peer groups.

This was almost twenty years ago, but I remember it so clearly because on that day I began, as never before, to see priesthood activity in a broader context. It helped me move to a much wider definition of "Church work" and to see *all* kinds of community and social work as priesthood activity.

I have found it helpful to think deeply about my own life mission and about each of my roles in fulfilling it. It's been useful to me to think in terms of two broad roles—first, as a son of God and also of Christ through the gospel covenant, and second, as a priesthood holder. My priesthood roles become priesthood *stewardship* roles—family (husband, father, grandfather, brother, uncle), neighbor (ward, stake, community), teacher, writer, business leader, friend. The Spirit helps me understand how to magnify the callings, or stewardships, that lie outside my Church responsibilities.

Basic Level— Personal Initiatives	Advanced Level— Enlarging Service Initiatives
1. Offer daily, listening prayers of faith.	1. Build strong human relationships through profound listening, affirming, and caring service.
2. Ponder the scriptures daily to feast on the words and love of Jesus Christ. ("Give us this day our daily bread.")	2. Teach and testify, by the Spirit, of Christ and his atoning sacrifice.
3. Exercise "repentance unto baptism," or partake of the sacrament worthily (obeying "general commandments"— becoming perfect *in* Christ).	3. Forgive all others and rebuild wounded relationships, as guided by the Spirit (obeying "personal commandments").
4. Magnify priesthood and Church callings.	4. Magnify "outside-the-Church" callings as given by the Spirit.

THE RESTORATION OF THE KEYS OF SALVATION

WHAT IS THE WORK I SHOULD DO IN LIFE?

CHAPTER 8

THE FIFTH EVENT: THE RESTORATION OF THE KEYS OF SALVATION

WHAT IS THE WORK I SHOULD DO IN LIFE?

A FEW MONTHS AFTER THE CHURCH was organized, Joseph Smith received a revelation instructing him to gather the Latter-day Saints in Ohio. "And there," the Lord said, "you shall be endowed with power from on high" (D&C 38:32). Once the headquarters of the Church was established in Kirtland, Ohio, the Prophet was commanded to build a temple in that place (see D&C 88:119). Despite poverty and tribulation, the Saints constructed the Kirtland Temple over a period of several years, and it was finally dedicated on March 27, 1836. In his dedicatory prayer, the Prophet asked the Lord "to accept of this house . . . that the Son of Man might have a place to manifest himself to his people" (D&C 109:4–5). Some of the most powerful spiritual manifestations in the history of the Church took place in the Kirtland Temple during the weeks surrounding the dedicatory services. This period has often been referred to as a time of Pentecostal experiences.

One week after the dedication, on Sunday, April 3, 1836, Joseph Smith and Oliver Cowdery knelt together in the temple and sought the Lord in "solemn and silent prayer" (*History of the Church,* 2:435). As they arose from their knees, Jesus Christ appeared to them and said, "Lift up your heads and rejoice. Let the hearts of your brethren rejoice, and let the hearts of all my people rejoice, who have, with their might, built this house to my name. For behold, I have accepted this house, and . . . the hearts of thousands and tens of thousands shall greatly rejoice in consequence of the blessings which shall be poured out . . . in this house. And the fame of this house shall spread to foreign lands; and this is the beginning of the blessing which shall be poured out upon the heads of my people" (D&C 110:5–10).

Immediately following this remarkable vision, Moses, Elias, and Elijah appeared in succession and committed to Joseph and Oliver "the keys of this dispensation" (D&C 110:11–16). I believe that the delivery of these keys was the main purpose for which the Kirtland Temple was built.

Elder Bruce R. McConkie gave an elegant summary of these events:

> Moses, who in the majesty of the Melchizedek Priesthood led enslaved Israel out of Egyptian bondage into their promised Palestine, brings back those very keys. These keys empower mortals to gather the lost sheep of Israel from the Egypt of the world, and bring them to their promised Zion, where the scales of enslaving darkness will drop from their eyes. . . .
>
> The man Elias brings back "the gospel of Abraham," the great Abrahamic covenant whereby the faithful receive promises of eternal increase, promises that through celestial marriage their eternal posterity shall be as numerous as the sands upon the seashore or as the stars in heaven for multitude. Elias gives the promise—

received of old by Abraham, Isaac, and Jacob—that in modern men and in their seed all generations shall be blessed. And we are now offering the blessings of Abraham, Isaac, and Jacob to all who will receive them.

Elijah brings back the keys of the sealing power, the power that enables men now living, as it was with Peter of old, to bind on the earth below and have their acts sealed everlastingly in the heavens above. (See D&C 110:11–16.)

Because Elijah came, the baptisms we perform on earth will have efficacy, virtue, and force in eternity. In literal reality they give us membership in the earthly kingdom which is the Church, and in the heavenly kingdom which is the celestial realm where God and Christ are ("The Keys of the Kingdom," *Ensign*, May 1983, 21).

Through the power and authority restored by these three ancient prophets, the Church is literally changing the world. Exactly as Daniel prophesied, "the stone . . . cut out of the mountain without hands" is rolling forth to fill the whole earth (see Daniel 2:34–35, 44–45). It is happening today. Not only are we witnessing it; we are *participating* in it. Thus, the question "What is the work we should do as citizens of God's kingdom?" is answered by the fifth transcendent event of the Restoration.

"The Keys of the Gathering of Israel"

When Moses appeared to Joseph Smith and Oliver Cowdery in the Kirtland Temple, he "committed unto [them] the keys of the gathering of Israel from the four parts of the earth, and the leading of the ten tribes from the land of the north" (D&C 110:11). A gathering is a coming together. It's through these keys that missionary work is accomplished throughout the world, and by this power the Jews and the ten tribes will eventually return to their homeland. But

I also believe that the same keys infuse *all* of Israel with a spirit of gathering. When the Saints come together to worship on the Sabbath day, and when we gather in our homes for family home evening and family prayer, I see that as part of the gathering process.

Years ago, when I served as a regional representative, I was assigned to work with several stakes in Salt Lake City. The presidency and the high council of one of those stakes invited me to join them in the Salt Lake Temple to participate in a special prayer for their stake members. The prayer meeting itself lasted only fifteen or twenty minutes, but it took more than four hours for me to "gather" to that event: to travel to and from the temple, change into the proper clothing, and so forth. Such meetings are no longer held in the temples, but it was a powerful teaching experience—four hours for a short prayer. It struck me that prayer is one of the most important things we can ever do.

Sometimes I've been so busy at home that I haven't wanted to take time to gather my children for family prayer. But then I've remembered that temple meeting, and I've realized that we must do it. We must kneel together as a family, both morning and night, to give thanks to God and pray for his Spirit and blessings to attend us. We simply must not become so hurried and rushed that we neglect it. And we should ask each family member if he or she has any special needs that ought to be addressed in the prayer; otherwise it has less meaning and may become almost a social ritual. No matter what, we must pay the price to gather for family prayer every day. Earnest prayer teaches us that the real "leverage activity" in life is to form a partnership with the living God.

"The Gospel of Abraham"

Immediately after Moses delivered the keys of the gathering in the Kirtland Temple, "Elias appeared, and committed the dispensation of the gospel of Abraham, saying that in us and our seed all generations after us should be blessed" (D&C 110:12).

We're not sure about the identity of this prophet, because *Elias* is used as both a name and a title, and in the scriptures it refers to several people. But we know that he restored the authority and promises given to Abraham. Known as the "father of the faithful," Abraham was promised by the Lord that all nations of the earth would be blessed through his seed (see Genesis 12:3; 22:18; 26:4; Abraham 2:9–11). This birthright descended from Abraham through Isaac, Jacob, Joseph, and Ephraim. Most of the members of the Church today are from Joseph and Ephraim. What is their role? It is to provide the moral and spiritual leadership that will transform the entire world. We can do this by the very way that we live, but it also requires that we bear witness to the truth and administer the ordinances of the priesthood.

The Lord promised Abraham, "I will multiply thy seed as the stars of the heaven, and as the sand which is upon the sea shore" (Genesis 22:17). And he has extended the same promise to the faithful Latter-day Saints: *"This promise is yours also, because ye are of Abraham. . . .* Go ye, therefore, and do the works of Abraham; enter ye into my law and ye shall be saved" (D&C 132:31–32; emphasis added). Thus Elias's appearance in the Kirtland Temple has to do with perfecting the Saints through the establishment of the eternal family structure.

Restoration of the Sealing Power

Elijah came next and restored the sealing power. The Prophet Joseph Smith wrote, "After this vision [of Elias] had closed, another great and glorious vision burst upon us; for Elijah the prophet, who was taken to heaven without tasting death, stood before us, and said: Behold, the time has fully come, which was spoken of by the mouth of Malachi—testifying that he [Elijah] should be sent, before the great and dreadful day of the Lord come—to turn the hearts of the fathers to the children, and the children to the fathers, lest the whole earth be smitten with a curse" (D&C 110:13–15).

"Why should he send Elijah?" asked President Spencer W. Kimball. "Because he held the keys of the authority to administer in all the ordinances of the priesthood, and without the authority that is given, the ordinances could not be administered in righteousness" ("Strengthening the Family—the Basic Unit of the Church," *Ensign,* May 1978, 47).

President Joseph Fielding Smith explained that "Elijah came to restore . . . the keys of binding and sealing on earth and in heaven of all the ordinances and principles pertaining to the salvation of man, that they may thus become valid in the celestial kingdom of God." He said that these keys include the authority to seal or bind families together for eternity, thus creating new kingdoms that will last forever: "Through the power of this priesthood which Elijah bestowed, husband and wife may be sealed, or married for eternity; children may be sealed to their parents for eternity; thus the family is made eternal, and death does not separate the members. This is the great principle that will save the world from utter destruction" (*Doctrines of Salvation* 2:117–18).

The concept of a universal plan of salvation appeals to a deep sense of justice in the human soul, to a deep sense of eternal fairness. In a similar way, most people find the idea of eternal families to be natural and appealing. These ideas are directly related to the missions of Elijah and Elias.

The sealing power restored by Elijah pertains to both the living and the dead, and it is this power that makes it possible for us to administer temple ordinances by proxy for those who have passed away. I don't think we have any idea of the pressure and influence exerted from the other side of the veil to get this work accomplished. For example, I believe that is a part of what drove the priesthood revelation received by President Spencer W. Kimball in 1978. Many who live in the spirit world are ready for the ordinances of the gospel, and we must perform that work.

One woman writes of a dream she had that demonstrated that truth to her:

> I had a dream that I was back in my childhood home, and it was night and dark outside. There was a sliding glass door that opened up, and in walked a little boy, unclothed except for a little brief, and he was starving and cold and lost. I looked at him like any mother would, with feelings of compassion and horror. I couldn't understand how his family could have abandoned him. I felt that I had to get him some help. I asked, "What's your name? Where's your family?" He said—well, I thought he said—"McAlister McKinzey." So I started looking up on the ward list for a family named McKinzey, thinking I needed to get the authorities, to get some help for this child. And then I woke up.
>
> Because I'd had enough experience with such dreams, I always kept a notebook by the side of my bed. So I scrawled out McAlister McKinzey, and then I went back to sleep.
>
> The next morning, when I woke up, I immediately understood the interpretation of the dream: There was a soul who was lost from his family and needed to be reunited and to receive the blessings of the gospel. I went down to look in my database, thinking that I had never heard of any McKinzeys in my line, but when I searched

the index I landed on one McKenzie. And his name was Alexander McKenzie.

Then I knew the interpretation crystal clear. He came to me as a lost little boy because he was lost—he was abandoned by his family. He had married into one of my pioneer lines but had never joined the Church. He died as an old man, but things often come symbolically in dreams, so he came to me as a child because spiritually he was a child. His progression was stopped and he was like a child. And he was lost and abandoned by his family because everybody else in his family was taken care of, but nobody had ever done his work. He was unclothed because he needed the ordinances of the temple, and to be endowed with power. And he was starving because he was hungering and thirsting for righteousness, but he couldn't be filled with the Holy Ghost, because he didn't have that ordinance.

It was a really busy week for me, but I thought, if this had come through the power of the Holy Ghost, which it surely had, and Heavenly Father had allowed it to come *this* week, *this* night, then I couldn't treat it any less than if a starving little unclothed child were standing at my front porch. And I would never say to that child, "Go away until next week. I'll get to you next week. I know you're starving. I know you're lost. I know you're frightened, but I can't right now." I put aside things on my schedule, and with very little time I went to the library. I found his records right away. Everything I needed to do his work was there, and I found it all within a couple of hours. I had the name submitted to the temple that day, and we had all this man's work done for him the next day.

That night I had another dream. I saw a little girl coming to me just overjoyed and thrilled. I saw her coming through a tunnel down at me to say, "Thank you." And I think that little girl represented his wife. Now the two of them could continue to progress and go forward together. And so, to me, the beauty of that is the poignancy of how important this work really is.

I also believe that this concept of redeeming the dead is one of the strongest evidences of the truthfulness of the restored gospel. I don't know of a more powerful or appealing missionary approach with fair-minded people than this doctrine. In my professional work, I'm involved with many Christians of other faiths. When I have the appropriate opportunity, I ask them if they honestly believe that Jesus Christ is the only name under heaven by which man can be saved (see Acts 4:12). They always say yes. Then I ask them, "Since most of the human race will live and die without ever hearing the name of Christ, what will happen to them?" They basically tell me that they don't know the answer, so I ask a third question: "How would you like to learn about the plan God has established to save *all* of his children?"

Except for the Lord's church, there is no organization or program anywhere that even claims the existence of such a plan. It is a plan so magnificent, so comprehensive, and so universal that it staggers the imagination. It is the only plan that is consistent with the perfect justice of God. And just as Christ's sacrifice for all mankind was vicarious, the sacrifice that we make when we go into the temple and perform vicarious labor for those who are beyond the veil enables us to become, in a sense, "saviours . . . on mount Zion" (Obadiah 1:21).

As with other sacrifices, blessings attend the work we perform for our ancestors and others in the temple. A woman who was seeking for a spiritual gift describes how she was guided to obtain it:

One time I was pouring out my heart in prayer for a particular gift of the Spirit. That night I dreamed that I saw my grandfather who had been deceased about two years. He was looking through his wallet for a couple of lost phone numbers, a couple of lost names. In the dream I was looking over his shoulder, trying to help him. And in the background in another room, where I couldn't see who the person was, a man whom I knew to be a member of our extended family was preaching this incredible sermon about this gift of the Spirit that I was seeking.

Then I woke up, and I just instantly knew what it meant. I knew that the Lord was linking those two things. If I would help my grandfather find those two names, then I would be given that spiritual gift.

The next morning I went downstairs and looked through my grandfather's things, which I would not normally have done, because I thought his line had been thoroughly researched already. But knowing that the Lord had sent me there, I knew that I would find something. I started with my grandfather's immediate family. He had six brothers, just one of whom was still living, and that brother was a temple worker. Glancing down the page, I realized that two of the brothers had gone inactive and had never had their endowments or their sealings done. I called my mom and asked, "Is it possible that they didn't take care of their brothers?" She said, "Well, I don't know. Call Uncle Ed at the Provo Temple." And I called him, and he said, "You know, I don't think we ever did."

I am quite certain that probably the very day the final

work had been completed, I received in a significant and obvious way the endowment in my life of that gift of the Spirit that I had been seeking.

No Separation of the Sacred and the Secular

Enough keys and powers were restored in the Kirtland Temple to literally save the *entire* human race. When Moses, Elias, and Elijah appeared on April 3, 1836, they gave Joseph Smith and Oliver Cowdery the authority and direction to carry out the three fundamental purposes of the Lord's latter-day kingdom: proclaiming the gospel, perfecting the Saints, and redeeming the dead. In a sense, it was the first priesthood executive committee meeting held in this dispensation.

In reality, these three purposes are simply three different aspects of the mission of the Church, which is to "invite all to come unto Christ" (D&C 20:59) "and be perfected in him" (Moroni 10:32). This whole concept of bringing people to Christ can be encompassed in a single word—*Zion.* The scriptures tell us that Zion consists of "the pure in heart" (D&C 97:21). And Zion is more than an individual; it is a family, a community, a geographic region, a civilization that has developed an immunity against the influence of the evil one. It is a millennial culture.

It's important to realize that the threefold mission of the Church blends temporal and spiritual activities together. This essentially tells us that there is no separation at all between the sacred and the secular. In Mormonism, everything is sacred. If all that we do is truly consecrated to the building of God's kingdom and the establishment of Zion, there is no such thing as secular work. The Lord has said, "All things unto me are spiritual, and not at any time have I given . . . a law which was temporal" (D&C 29:34). We should have the same perspective in everything we do. When

President Hinckley announced the inspired creation of the Perpetual Education Fund in the Priesthood Session of general conference of April 2001 ("Key to Opportunity"), everyone could sense the Lord's concern for the education and earning power of His children in providing for their families and building God's kingdom.

In the words of President David O. McKay, "Every noble impulse, every unselfish expression of love; every brave suffering for the right; every surrender of self to something higher than self; every loyalty to an ideal; every unselfish devotion to principle; every helpfulness to humanity; every act of self-control; every fine courage of the soul, undefeated by pretense or policy, but by being, doing, and living of good for the very good's sake—that is spirituality" ("Something Higher Than Self," in *Speeches of the Year*, October 12, 1965, 4–5).

Some people worry about "overdoing the church work." But what is church work? It goes far beyond the ward and the stake; in fact, it includes every stewardship in our lives. Believing that our temporal work is not part of our church work is a false paradigm. It's a social concept that comes from the scarcity mentality and causes people to compartmentalize their lives.

In a letter to priesthood leaders throughout the United States dated January 15, 1998, the First Presidency of the Church encouraged the Saints to be involved in their communities:

> We wish to reiterate the divine counsel that members "should be anxiously engaged in a good cause, and do many things of their own free will, and bring to pass much righteousness," while using gospel principles as a guide and while cooperating with other like-minded individuals (D&C 58:27). . . . We urge members of the Church to be full participants in political, governmental, and community affairs.

Clearly, the Lord is interested in having us contribute all that we can to the good of the world. This cannot be done if we limit our activities to the confines of Church programs.

At one time I was working with several stakes of the Church to find a regional welfare adviser. I spoke with one stake president about a man who seemed well qualified for the calling. The stake president said, "Well, he's a very good man, but the problem is that he doesn't come out to the stake welfare farm on Saturdays when the rest of us are there." I asked what the man did on Saturdays and learned that he sold real estate. I said, "Oh, you mean he's on his *family* welfare farm." The stake president wasn't sure what I meant, so I asked him, "Which do you think would be the greater neglect, the stake welfare farm or his family welfare farm? He can probably do both, but if he feels that he needs to give his energies to the family welfare farm on Saturdays, he can come to the stake welfare farm on a different day. His profession is real estate, and that's his family welfare farm. The Lord has said that 'if any provide not for his own, and specially for those of his own house, he hath denied the faith, and is worse than an infidel' [1 Timothy 5:8]."

We should be involved in many welfare activities, but the family welfare farm is a higher obligation. Several years ago at a large regional meeting, President Gordon B. Hinckley was asked a question about our priorities in life, and he basically said that under God we should put our families first, then our employment, and then our ward and stake callings.

For several years I accompanied General Authorities to stake conferences when they called new stake presidencies. As they conducted the interviews that are part of that process, I noticed that they always felt it was important that these men were taking care of their families and their temporal affairs, and had good reputations for doing so, because they were setting an example for the entire stake.

President Harold B. Lee taught that "learning by faith requires the bending of the whole soul through worthy living to become attuned to the Holy Spirit of the Lord" (*Stand Ye in Holy Places,* 358–59). Such faithfulness is perhaps even more urgently needed today, as we see the world becoming increasingly ripened in wickedness and evil. President Boyd K. Packer, speaking to the J. Reuben Clark Law Society in a worldwide broadcast from the Conference Center in February 2004, stated, "The world is spiraling downward at an ever-quickening pace. I am sorry to tell you it will not get better. . . . I know of nothing in the history of the church or in the history of the world to compare with our present circumstances. Nothing happened in Sodom and Gomorrah which exceeds the wickedness and depravity which surrounds us now. . . .

"Sodom and Gomorrah was localized. It is now spread across the world, wherever the Church is. The first line of defense—the home—is crumbling. Surely you can see what the adversary is about. We are now exactly where the prophets warned we would be."

President Packer went on to enumerate the long list of vices from 2 Timothy 3:1–7 that the apostle Paul warned would afflict people in the last days, saying "check" after each one (see Larry Weist, "World spiraling down, lawyers told," *Deseret Morning News,* February 29, 2004, B3). The implications of this frightening picture for the family are startling indeed. However, a few months later, in general conference, President Packer stated, "The moral values upon which civilization itself must depend spiral downward at an ever-increasing pace. Nevertheless, *I do not fear the future.*" He went on to say: "If you will accept it in your mind and cradle it in your feelings, a knowledge of the restored gospel and a testimony of Jesus Christ can spiritually immunize your children. One thing is very clear: the safest place and the best protection against the moral and spiritual diseases is a stable home and family. This has always been true; it will be true forever. We must keep that foremost in our minds" ("Do Not Fear," *Ensign,* May 2004, 77; italics added.)

Church Work Is Family Work

Many people have the idea that the family is separate from the Church, when in fact the family *is* the Church. I'm trying to train my children not to use the word *church* when they talk about going to a ward meeting or activity. We go to Sunday School, Primary, priesthood meeting, and so forth, but the Church's basic organizational unit is the family. President Harold B. Lee explained that "the priesthood [and auxiliary] programs operate in support of the home. . . . Both the revelations of God and the learning of men tell us how crucial the home is in shaping the individual's total life experience. . . . Much of what we do organizationally, then, is *scaffolding,* as we seek to build the individual, and we must not mistake the scaffolding for the soul" (*Stand Ye in Holy Places,* 309; emphasis added).

Elder M. Russell Ballard made the same point in a recent general conference of the Church. He said that "the family is where the foundation of personal, spiritual growth is built and nurtured; the Church, then, is the scaffolding that helps support and strengthen the family" ("Feasting at the Lord's Table," *Ensign,* May 1996, 81).

Under the influence of the Holy Ghost, a person begins to see that all truth is integrated together; there is no separation of sacred and secular things at all. From this perspective flows a whole new conception of life. For instance, Sunday becomes a preparation for our principal church work, which begins on Monday morning. The real activity of the priesthood is right in the home, because that's where the modeling and mentoring and most of the moral teaching take place. That's where a person begins to develop a sense of security and a basis for physical, intellectual, social, emotional, and spiritual growth.

A few years ago, someone in our stake asked me whether my wife, Sandra, could help with a certain project. He said, "We don't want to overburden her if she's too busy. Does she have any church callings?"

I answered, "Yes, she does."

"How many?"

"Thirteen."

He looked surprised and said, "I've never heard of anyone having thirteen callings. What are they?"

"Cynthia, Maria, Stephen, Sean, David . . ."

Before I could list the rest of our nine children and myself, he said, "Actually, I meant *church* callings."

"Oh, you mean jobs on the scaffolding? She's also serving as a member of the stake Young Women presidency, as a teacher in the Relief Society, and in one other calling in the ward."

"Yes, that's what I meant."

Then I asked him, "Do you think our daughter Colleen would be the equivalent of a Relief Society lesson?" We talked about the hours Sandra devoted to her ward and stake callings every month, and the time and attention she devoted to me and each of our children. I told him that I saw the family as part of the Church—even the foundation of the Church—and that I understood that's what the Brethren had encouraged us to do.

Because of our social conditioning, it takes time to break down these artificial divisions between the family and the Church.

I remember yelling at my children one Sunday, trying to get them to church on time. Then I suddenly thought, *Here I am, standing in church, yelling at my family to run onto the scaffolding so that we can learn how to love and talk with each other!* I had completely confused the issue.

Before the Church introduced the consolidated meeting schedule, we used to have an hour or so between priesthood meeting and Sunday School. Our home was only about five minutes away, but I remember thinking that it would be easier to stay at the meetinghouse so I wouldn't have to deal with the children. One time I did stay, and all the men were just standing around having gospel discussions while our wives were struggling to get our families ready for Sunday School. I realized that I was wrong, and that I had to go back and help Sandra with our nine active children, because the real church work was at home.

It took many years for me to internalize this concept, but I was educated in the role of the home through my service as a regional representative. As I sat at the feet of the General Authorities and traveled with them to conferences, I could see what they were teaching, and it gradually began to seep into me. For instance, on one occasion Elder A. Theodore Tuttle was training the regional representatives in the state of Utah. He asked us to encourage the stake presidents to begin and end their meetings on time. Then he said something like this: "It could be that one of those high councilors has a date at nine o'clock to take his wife out for a malt, and nothing they could talk about in that meeting is as sacred as that." He became very emotional as he said this to us; it was a powerful teaching moment that I have never forgotten.

When I watch my daughter play basketball or go skiing with my son, I'm doing church work. I've sometimes missed weekday ward and stake meetings to do that kind of church work. That doesn't mean we shouldn't spend a lot of time in ward and stake callings. I believe we should spend a good part of our lives on the scaffolding, helping other people and modeling to our own children the importance of being dynamically involved in building the kingdom of God. But our highest callings are in our families, not in the ward or stake.

When we say that church work is primarily family work, we should think not only in terms of our immediate families but also in terms of the intergenerational family. For instance, one way to ensure that our families are contributing to the mission of the Church is to establish missionary projects, welfare projects, Perpetual Education Fund projects, and family history and temple projects within the extended family. By this means the powerful modeling of the Church and its programs can penetrate and strengthen the eternal family organization, and we can work together to accomplish the Lord's purposes.

Family Life: An Apprenticeship for Becoming Perfect Like Christ

Many people neglect their family responsibilities in the name of ward and stake duties. Scaffolding activity is easy by comparison, because it allows us to avoid many of the deeper emotional forces that require attention in the home. But again, home is where the real church work is done. The truth is that we should be even more concerned about our spouses and children, our parents, our brothers and sisters, our in-laws, and our other relatives than we are about our Relief Society and priesthood quorum members.

I once worked with a priesthood leader who admitted that he kept himself busy doing "church work" to escape from family responsibilities. He said it was much easier for him to do that than refuel his deteriorating relationship with his wife or deal with the messy, frustrating problems his children were having. He was involved in a lot of leadership meetings where they talked about proclaiming the gospel, perfecting the Saints, and redeeming the dead, but his own family was emotionally and spiritually languishing. In fact, his children were growing up without experiencing even the first event of the Restoration on a personal level. They had no true sense of their own identity or of their relationship with Heavenly Father, and the resulting behavioral problems were so difficult that their father preferred to do "church work." He was unaware that the family is the very foundation of the Church and that his highest leadership responsibility was in his home.

I had the opportunity to be with President Harold B. Lee one time when we were setting apart a new stake presidency in California. He asked the stake president's wife to stand up, and then he said to her husband, "The most important church work you will ever do is with this woman in your home." The man responded, "I know how important she is. She's been a great support." President Lee looked at him and spoke with greater emphasis: "You did not hear what I said to you. *The most important church work you will ever do is with this woman.* Remember that."

Family work is by far the most important work. It's also the toughest work emotionally, because our homes are where we're stretched the most, where we're the most open and vulnerable. I'm convinced that the deepest tests in mortality are family tests. Marriage and family life are more intimate, more constant, more intense, and more demanding than any other stewardship.

At the same time, the home is the most profound source of personal growth and development. It's where we overcome our weaknesses and self-doubts and develop true inner strength. It's where we practice love, giving, and sacrifice. It's where we learn to create Zion. That's why family life is an apprenticeship for god-hood. It's the most challenging and problematic of all mortal experiences, but also the most powerful and rewarding. The highest level of sanctification is learned in the intimacy of family relationships, because all the natural tendencies surface there and can't be hidden. Thus if we can bring the power of the gospel into our homes, we can grow at a level that will eventually enable us to receive the fullness of the Father.

Faithful to the End

The three basic purposes of the Church should consume our efforts until the end of our mortal lives. There's not much place in the Lord's kingdom for "retirement." In fact, the idea of retire-ment is, in my opinion, a sick, secular notion. We may retire from an occupation, but we retire to serve missions on both sides of the veil. If we study the literature in the field of stress, we find that the key to staying healthy and vibrant is to stay involved in mean-ingful projects that continually excite and energize us. Such proj-ects actually retard the degenerative forces in the body and strengthen the immune system; they can literally give us ten or more years of life. I think that's one reason why many of the General Authorities are so active at an advanced age.

Since life is not a career but a mission, there's no better retire-ment concept than the gospel: the work goes on, we're in a con-stant learning mode, and we continue to grow to the very end of our lives. Every person has enormous capacity, and we must not lose our opportunity to contribute as we get older.

Our role as Latter-day Saints is to push forward the mission of the Church all of our days. For us, retirement is missionary work, priesthood and Relief Society work, family history and temple work, and community work. To bless other people is what our mission in life is all about. It will renew our bodies, our minds, and our spirits; not only will we live longer, but we will also enjoy a higher quality of life. A life of consecration may require that we give up a few personal pleasures, but it will produce tremendous joy.

Internalizing the Fifth Event

Understanding the threefold mission of the Church, it is easy to see many worthy tasks in which we might be engaged. Anything relating to proclaiming the gospel, perfecting the Saints, and redeeming the dead could be considered a basic initiative for the fifth event. I suggest that special attention be paid to attending to "temporal" matters, or family concerns, as an important aspect of this threefold mission.

This basic level of initiative might be taken a step further by "bending your whole soul" in righteous living, seeking in all things to bring about a Zion society by building up the kingdom of God on the earth. This is the path to sanctification, or becoming perfect *like* Christ.

It is in this context that one of the most universal human struggles often surfaces. I refer to the tendency of almost all of us to compete and compare. In fact, I believe there are five interlinked, metastasizing cancers common to the "natural man" that undermine and even destroy peace and happiness: *criticizing, complaining, competing, comparing,* and *contending.* Even covenanted, temple-attending people sometimes compare and judge others based on callings or family size or worldly achievements. Christ's own disciples, who knew his nature and his generosity, who understood the blessings promised to them through the gospel, fought for the primary position of leadership, as if occupying the seat on Christ's right hand would make that disciple more important.

Bending our whole souls in righteous living, to overcome

such worldly tendencies, is hard work. It is uncomfortable to examine ourselves for weaknesses that have been a source of comfort and a sense of superiority. Most of us prefer to look outside ourselves for the roots of our problems. We blame, complain, and criticize others' behaviors, ideas, or systems in an attempt to fix what may really be a problem rooted deep within ourselves. Perhaps we do not realize just how deeply embedded these feelings are until we reveal ourselves in a moment of pressure. C. S. Lewis described his feelings this way:

> When I come to my evening prayers and try to reckon up the sins of the day, nine times out of ten the most obvious one is some sin against charity; I have sulked or snapped or sneered or snubbed or stormed. And the excuse that immediately springs to mind is that the provocation was so sudden or unexpected; I was caught off my guard, I had not time to collect myself. . . . Surely what a man does when he is taken off his guard is the best evidence for what sort of man he is. Surely what pops out before the man has time to put on a disguise is the truth. If there are rats in the cellar you are most likely to see them if you go in very suddenly. But the suddenness does not create rats; it only prevents them from hiding. In the same way the suddenness of provocation does not make me an ill-tempered man; it only shows me what an ill-tempered man I am (*Mere Christianity,* 164–65).

How do we overcome these tendencies to sin against charity? The power of choice is the key. Through our human endowments of self-awareness and conscience, we become conscious of areas of weakness, areas for improvement, areas of talents, areas that need to be changed or eliminated from our lives. By these endowments we also become conscious of Christ and his powers. Then, as we recognize and use our imagination and independent will to act on that awareness, making promises, making covenants, and even setting goals and being true to them, we gradually build the strength of Christ's nature and character into our being. This is what is meant by "bending our whole souls in righteous living." This is the key to building the kingdom of God on the earth and becoming a Zion people.

Basic Level— Personal Initiatives	Advanced Level— Enlarging Service Initiatives
1. Offer daily, listening prayers of faith.	1. Build strong human relationships through profound listening, affirming, and caring service.
2. Ponder the scriptures daily to feast on the words and love of Jesus Christ. ("Give us this day our daily bread.")	2. Teach and testify, by the Spirit, of Christ and his atoning sacrifice.
3. Exercise "repentance unto baptism," or partake of the sacrament worthily (obeying "general commandments"— becoming perfect *in* Christ).	3. Forgive all others and rebuild wounded relationships, as guided by the Spirit (obeying "personal commandments").
4. Magnify priesthood and Church callings.	4. Magnify "outside-the-Church" callings as given by the Spirit.
5. Give honest, diligent service in prayerfully seeking referrals, attending to "temporal" matters, and worshipping in the temple.	**5. Seeing all things as stewardship, "bend your whole soul" in righteous living, in establishing Zion (becoming perfect *like* Christ).**

THE RESTORATION OF THE TEMPLE ORDINANCES

WHY DID GOD BRING ABOUT THE RESTORATION?

CHAPTER 9

THE SIXTH EVENT: THE RESTORATION OF THE TEMPLE ORDINANCES

WHY DID GOD BRING ABOUT THE RESTORATION?

THE RESTORATION OF THE TEMPLE ordinances was really a process rather than an event. The Lord gave these ordinances to the Prophet Joseph Smith through a series of revelations from 1836 to 1843, "line upon line" and "precept upon precept." For example, only a small part of the temple ceremony was administered in the Kirtland Temple, and no ordinances for the dead were ever performed there.

But after the Church was established in Nauvoo, Illinois, the Lord said, "I command you, all ye my saints, to build a house unto me; . . . for therein are the keys of the holy priesthood ordained, that you may receive honor and glory. . . . And verily I say unto you, let this house be built unto my name, *that I may reveal mine ordinances therein unto my people;* for I design to reveal unto my church things which have been kept hid from before the foundation of the world . . . that you may prove yourselves unto me that ye are faithful in all things whatsoever I command you, that I may bless you, and crown you with honor, immortality, and eternal life" (D&C 124:31, 34, 40–41, 55; emphasis added).

So strongly did the Lord feel about the construction of the Nauvoo Temple that he told the Saints they would be "rejected as a church" if they failed to build it within a certain period of time (D&C 124:31–32). Elder John A. Widtsoe, a former member of the Council of the Twelve, once said that "the main concern of the Prophet Joseph Smith in the restoration of the Gospel in these latter days was the founding, building, and completion of temples in which the ordinances 'hid from before the foundation of the world' might be given. In fact, the Lord declared repeatedly to the Prophet that unless temples were built and used, the plan of salvation could neither be in full operation nor fully accomplished" ("Temple Worship," *Utah Genealogical and Historical Magazine,* April 1921, 53). To understand why this is so, we must consider the real purpose of temples.

What Is the Restoration All About?

It is through the ordinances of the temple that the Lord has revealed his ultimate purpose in bringing about the Restoration. What is the true significance of the temple? The temple is where the eternal family is created, and it is where the fullness of the Father is given.

Everything associated with the temple endowment—the preparatory ordinances, the instructions, the covenants, and all the rest—leads to the sealing room, where we receive "the new and everlasting covenant of marriage" (D&C 131:2) for time and all eternity. This sacred ordinance creates the eternal family, literally a new kingdom, that will ultimately be presided over by "kings and queens, and priests and priestesses" (*The Teachings of*

Spencer W. Kimball, 331). That's what exaltation is. Baptism is the ordinance of *salvation* in the celestial kingdom, but temple marriage is the ordinance of *exaltation.* And through the sealing power, families can be bound together through the generations to create an unending linkage of our Heavenly Father's children.

The Proclamation on the Family is, in my judgment, the finest, the most inspired, and the most needed revelation from God through his apostles and prophets ever given on the subject of the family. It was read by President Gordon B. Hinckley as part of his message at the General Relief Society Meeting held September 23, 1995, just at the beginning of the flood of misconception and wickedness that is weakening the structure of family life throughout the entire world.

Study the Proclamation carefully with your family and with your grandchildren. Each sentence is pregnant with meaning; each phrase was carefully and prayerfully crafted and approved by the First Presidency and the Quorum of the Twelve Apostles. It will bear the deepest scrutiny and stand the utmost test of time. It is filled with God's doctrine, with God's paradigm of truth. It is light years ahead of the cumulative wisdom and knowledge of all of the researchers, scholars, academics, teachers, and leaders the world over.

The sequence in the Proclamation is most interesting and instructive. The first paragraph—who is giving it. The second paragraph—our creation as sons and daughters of God. The third paragraph—our premortal life and the plan of happiness. The fourth paragraph—the commandment to Adam and Eve to multiply and replenish the earth, still in force. The fifth paragraph—the means of creating mortal life is divinely appointed. The sixth paragraph—how parents are to raise their children. The seventh paragraph—the essence of happy family life. The eighth paragraph—a warning to those who violate these principles and their covenants.

The ninth paragraph—the call to citizens and government to promote the strengthening of the family as the fundamental unit of society. The entire Proclamation moves in orderly sequence from our relationship with God to our relationship with our families to our relationships in society.

The need to strengthen families is recognized well beyond the bounds of the Church. One institution, the Commission on Children at Risk, is made up of numerous noted scholars and expert authorities from throughout the country. This Commission has the task of investigating the social, moral, and spiritual foundations of children's well-being, evaluating the degree to which current practice and policy in the United States recognize those foundations, and making recommendations for the future. In its executive summary, the Commission reports "high and rising rates of depression, anxiety, attention deficit, conduct disorders, thoughts of suicide, and other serious mental, emotional, and behavioral problems among U.S. children and adolescents." And how is society dealing with these problems? "We are using medications and psychotherapies. We are designing more and more special programs for 'at risk' children. These approaches are necessary. But they are not enough. Why? Because programs of individual risk-assessment and treatment seldom encourage us, and can even prevent us, from recognizing as a society the broad *environmental* conditions that are contributing to growing numbers of suffering children."

The report goes on to ask, "What's causing the crisis?" Then it gives the answer: "In large measure, what's causing this crisis of American childhood is a lack of connectedness. We mean two kinds of connectedness—close connections to other people, and deep connections to moral and spiritual meaning.

"Where does this connectedness come from? It comes from

groups of people organized around certain purposes—what scholars call social institutions. *In recent decades, the U.S. social institutions that foster these two forms of connectedness for children have gotten significantly weaker.* That weakening, this report argues, is a major cause of the current mental and behavioral health crisis among U.S. children. . . .

"What can help most to solve the crisis are *authoritative communities.*

"Authoritative communities are groups that live out the types of connectedness that our children increasingly lack. They are groups of people who are committed to one another over time and who model and pass on at least part of what it means to be a good person and live a good life. Renewing and building them is the key to improving the lives of U.S. children and adolescents."

It's most interesting to see an honest scientific effort to understand the problems children face and to present recommendations for the solution. These are magnificently found in the restoration of the gospel and The Church of Jesus Christ of Latter-day Saints.

Eternal Family Relationships

Can you imagine a more "authoritative community" than the family? The perpetuation throughout eternity of this most basic institution is the reason for the existence of temples. Thus the temple is really a place of marriage. We sometimes tend to look at the temple ordinances separately because of our circumstances in life. For instance, a missionary may be endowed several years before he or she is married in the temple. And many members of the Church have no opportunity for temple marriage during mortality. (The prophets have taught that the Saints in that situation who stay in the gospel path will not be denied the blessing of eternal marriage in the resurrection.) But as we stand apart and place the temple ordinances in perspective, we realize that they are all in preparation for the marriage covenant, through which we are promised eternal life and "a continuation of the seeds forever and ever" (D&C 132:19). The Lord has said that those who remain faithful to this covenant "shall . . . be gods, because they have no end" (D&C 132:20). This is the eternal purpose for which he brought about the latter-day Restoration.

Why are marriage and family life so vitally important? I believe it is because they are an apprenticeship to becoming more like God and Christ. There is nothing else so demanding, so involving, so intimate, so relentless. Putting it simply, I think the family is a world of interdependency. People are often either dependent (relying on others to have their needs met) or independent (relying on themselves for everything). Interdependency, which implies a reliance on others paired with a willingness to act for oneself, taxes them to the utmost. Unless they have an interdependent relationship with God from experiencing the fruits of the first five events, it is as if they were trying to play golf with a tennis racket—or, even more ludicrous, tennis with a golf club. The tool is simply not suited to the challenge. Thus the need to rise up and accept responsibilities built into the marriage covenant and in the creation of the eternal family.

And a nuclear family (two generations) is simple compared to a multigenerational family. Why do you need to get involved with all of your in-laws, with all of your cousins, with all of your aunts and uncles, when your hands are so full with your own? This is what enlarges our capacities and helps us become more like our Heavenly Father, who has billions of spirit children and yet has the capacity to deal with them individually.

Nurturing an intergenerational family can be a difficult task, particularly when generations of dysfunction have damaged family relationships. I had a profound experience regarding this problem when I was invited to speak at a luncheon for the National Fatherhood Initiative Conference. I attended the first evening's dinner meeting and then had a breakfast with the president of the organization the next morning prior to my speech. At the breakfast, the president said to me that he had misgivings about the speech he had given the night before, in which he had described his own childhood in a profoundly dysfunctional home where there was considerable drug and child abuse, including beatings and other violent actions. His father had passed on, and he felt that he did not properly keep the commandment, "Honor thy father and thy mother."

I said to him, "The whole context and spirit of your speech was not denigrating toward your father. It was a realistic explanation of the situation that you were in and that you confronted. Now you are heading up an organization to help fathers assume their rightful role and to be responsible and committed and loving toward their children. So really, you're turning your experiences into a good. You're becoming a transition figure. You are a catalyst for change. You have stopped the transmission of the sins of earlier generations with yourself so that they will not be passed on to your children, and in that way you are blessing your father. You are honoring him by stopping the consequences of his transgressions going into future generations. He is now in the spirit world, and his heart is turning toward you, and your heart is turning toward him and toward your own children."

He sat there in wonder and amazement listening to this. He had never heard anything like it. He asked me to elaborate, so I told him about the mission of Elijah in the Old Testament, and also Malachi's prophecy that Elijah would return to the earth to turn the hearts of the children to their fathers and the hearts of the fathers to their children, that the whole earth might not be smitten with a curse. I said the curse would be in the form of breaking up those family associations and relationships, not allowing the full flowering to take place so that families are sealed together forever. He sat there with tears filling his eyes upon hearing this entirely new doctrine. I said, "You honored your father last night, and you honor your father as you continue this most noble work. You are full of the spirit of Elijah, who has returned to this earth in these latter days, and the spirit is flooding the world."

He responded, "I don't know what you were planning to say today, Stephen, but I would like to ask you to speak on what you have just told me, because most of the fathers in the audience feel somewhat like I do and have had similar kinds of experiences, and they too are what you call 'transition figures.' They need to hear an affirmation of the nobility of what they are attempting to do and the nobility of this work and organization. I think this will do more to inspire and motivate them to carry this spirit on throughout this country."

As the spirit of Elijah brings more and more people to the temple, turning hearts of children to fathers and fathers to children, I believe the Lord will send many noble children to earth as transition figures to heal the long-standing wounds in their families. Thus the work of the temple blesses all generations and strengthens the world by stopping unproductive cycles of sin.

"Endowed with Power from On High"

To be honest, I have to say there was a time when I often went to the temple out of a sense of duty. I attended regularly and had a nice experience, sometimes even a very inspirational experience. But it was not until I served as a mission president in

Ireland that the temple became the Lord's university to me—truly enlightening and energizing.

At that time, some of the missions in Great Britain were languishing. Our mission supervisor, Elder Mark E. Petersen of the Council of the Twelve, felt that the missionaries needed to be "endowed with power from on high" (D&C 105:11), so he permitted the mission presidents to take all the elders and sisters to London for a temple experience. He emphasized that our primary purpose was not to do work for the dead, as important as that was, but rather to prepare ourselves to do better missionary work.

We went twice a year and stayed for a full week each time. It would be difficult to do that today, but back then the Saints used the temple mostly on Friday evenings and Saturdays for their temple trips, and it wasn't very busy on weekdays. Thus the missionaries were allowed to be there from Monday through Friday morning. They were scheduled in three different groups, so each companionship was in London for about a day and a half.

We spent the whole day in the temple. We were not rushed; each elder and sister attended four or five sessions in a row and had thirty to sixty minutes between each session to reflect on the meaning of the endowment. In the evening, we let the missionaries decide whether to socialize and enjoy themselves at the manor house on the temple grounds; play basketball at a nearby stake center; take a tour or even see a clean play in London; or attend another session in the temple. Every night they chose another endowment—even though they knew they would be attending two more sessions the following morning before the next group of missionaries came in. This went on twice a year for two years. The missionaries always wanted to go back to the temple, because they were genuinely excited by the things they were learning there.

Little by little, the insights came. The key to it all was the time we spent in reflection, simply pondering the endowment and allowing light and knowledge to distill upon our souls "as the dews from heaven" (D&C 121:45). People have to train themselves to have "eyes to see, and ears to hear" (Deuteronomy 29:4). Joseph Smith said that "the things of God are of deep import; and time, and experience, and careful and ponderous and solemn thoughts can only find them out" (*Teachings of the Prophet Joseph Smith,* 137). We must get our minds deeply into the temple and refuse to be diverted by temporal or superficial things. If we will stay with it and keep returning for another experience, we will begin to understand what the temple is all about.

The effect this process had on us was so deep, so real, so profound that I don't have words to describe it. These moments of sublime spiritual insight were among the most significant experiences I have ever had; they gave me a new understanding of the temple and of life itself. And we did in fact receive an endowment of power that proved to be a tremendous blessing to our missionary work. It corrected our mental maps and enabled us to love people as never before. It quadrupled our convert baptisms in Ireland and led to a great turnaround in the missions of Great Britain. In addition, it helped bring about the conversion of the missionaries themselves.

Preparation Is the Key

It's vital that we prepare ourselves before we go to the temple—beginning with the very first time. President Spencer W. Kimball taught that the endowment is for those who are mature in the gospel:

> Because of the sacred nature of the endowment and the other ordinances performed in the temple, those who

go to the temple to receive them must be prepared and worthy. . . .

It is not proper to go to the temple for the purpose of getting the strength to live righteously, but rather [a person should] acquire the strength and determination to live the commandments so that there can be total worthiness when [he or she goes] to the temple (*The Teachings of Spencer W. Kimball*, 536–37).

Priesthood leaders can help those who are going to the temple for the first time by carefully preparing and educating them so that their expectations are congruent with what they're going to experience. But sometimes people go to the temple before they are fully prepared. Several years ago, a sister who was about to enter the mission field was interviewed by the president of the Missionary Training Center. During the interview she expressed a concern to him. "I hated the temple," she said. "I didn't understand what was going on, and I didn't agree with much of what I did understand."

The president listened carefully and let her express her feelings until she appeared to have said all that she wanted to. Then he calmly responded, "If that's the way you feel, then you shouldn't go on a mission."

This young sister looked surprised and asked, "Why do you say that? I'm not going to teach the temple; I'm going to teach people about Christ and how to live a happy life. What does the temple have to do with that?"

The president explained, "The temple is the embodiment of all that we are and all that we can be. If you don't have deep convictions about the temple, you can never really be a good missionary." He advised her that she would be excused from her classes the next day and asked her to spend the entire day in the temple. He challenged her to go there prayerfully and sincerely and to seek with all of her heart for spiritual understanding.

Late the next day, she returned to the president's office. She had attended three sessions in the temple and had spent a lot of time pondering and praying in the celestial room. Her countenance was recognizably different than it had been the day before. As she described her experience and her new feelings to the president, they both knew that she had been "endowed with power from on high" and was now ready to begin her missionary service.

Even those of us who were endowed many years ago need to prepare ourselves each time we go to the temple. As with the sacrament, the key to our temple experience is the *preparation* we bring to it. If we really want to tap into the deep spiritual reservoir of the Lord's house, we must focus our minds and hearts for a sustained period of time on the things that take place there.

The next time you plan to attend the temple, thoroughly prepare yourself before you go. If you're going with another person, agree with each other ahead of time that you'll help each other get ready for the experience. Pray, read scriptures or other writings about the temple, and think about what you're doing. Don't watch the news or other television programs or listen to worldly music. Just immerse yourself in this preparation. Don't let anything interrupt you during your drive to the temple, and don't talk about anything but the experience you're going to have.

As you enter the temple, be still and quiet. Have a prayerful, open mind. Don't be rushed; take off your watch. Silently get dressed, go into the chapel or waiting room, and hope that you'll have some reflective time there. During the entire time you're in the temple, have the expectation that God will reveal to you the answers to your prayers. You don't know when, but you know that he will—you just feel it.

I want to emphasize that we shouldn't get into a rush at all when we go to the temple. In other words, don't be efficient. Efficiency with God, with ourselves, or with other people is ineffective, especially when we're dealing with deep, jugular issues and problems. Oftentimes we rush to get here and there; we may rush through family prayer or some other sacred experience, or perhaps even miss it altogether. The temple teaches us that God's ways are not man's ways. Don't get efficient with important things. Have you ever been efficient with your spouse or one of your teenagers on a tough issue? Have you ever been efficient in your prayers? How did it go? The world is rushed, but the temple slows things down. What I'm suggesting is that we slow down long before we get to the temple.

Whenever possible, try to get a name that you can take through all of the temple ordinances, or attend at least two endowment sessions in a row so that you can experience the cumulative effect of becoming immersed in that heavenly environment. When you finish a session, stay in the celestial room and ponder your experience. If you're with a loved one, quietly share your feelings with each other. Stay focused; don't get into the world, and don't get into your personal problems too quickly. Just think about the endowment for a while—God's home, his way, how he prepares his children to receive truth, who Christ is, who we are, and so forth. As you reflect on these sacred things, your mind becomes more alert to what the Spirit can teach you, and you become eager to come back and learn more.

As you do this, you begin to take on the characteristics of those who live in an eternal culture, the Lord's culture. What is a culture? Simply, a culture is a shared value system. When people value similar things, their priorities are basically the same. If the assumptions they make about the nature of reality are basically the same, those become their culture, and that culture produces their behavior. It also produces a kind of lens through which they interpret other people's behavior and through which they interpret all of life.

Immerse Yourself in the Lord's Culture

Attending the temple is like being immersed in the Lord's culture for two or three or more hours. If we do it consistently, regularly, prayerfully, earnestly, sincerely, it starts to plant in us the Lord's lens, the outlook of a celestial culture. However, if we are not aware of the lens through which we interpret life, we may interpret our temple experiences through the cultural lens of our upbringing or our present situation.

Just to illustrate, efficiency is one of the high values of my world. It's not as high as effectiveness—effectiveness is doing the right things, but efficiency is doing the right things right, doing them quickly. I've even tried to be efficient in my temple worship in the way I organize to get there, dress rapidly, and hope that I don't have too long of a wait in the chapel. And even though I accept that the endowment session usually runs a little over an hour and a half, I'll often put my mind into an efficient state of trying to learn more about the endowment or even try to do two things at the same time mentally, then spend a few minutes in the celestial room, rush to get dressed, and then run off to some other activity.

But if you attend the temple faithfully, the culture of the temple starts to affect you, and you realize you can't force natural processes like the six days of creation—each one follows upon the previous one and builds on it. I've even found myself trying to be efficient in my prayers and in scripture reading and in lesson preparation and in teaching and in human interactions. But I learn over and over again, usually the hard way, that efficiency with

God, with others, and with self all fail. With people, with God, and with self, generally I have found that fast is slow and slow is fast. That is a hard lesson that I am continually relearning because efficiency is such a deep value in my life and in the culture I am immersed in. My hope, however, is that once I am aware of this cultural lens, I can take it into account and subordinate it to higher values. If I am not aware of it, then I am enslaved by it. But the temple can help us overcome our cultural shortsightedness and begin to understand the eternal view of our Father in Heaven.

"A House of Learning"

The temple is the place where heaven and earth touch. It is a place of revelation, where the fullness of the Holy Ghost dwells. It is the Lord's true university, where things long withheld from the children of men—the higher doctrines, the mysteries of godliness, the truths pertaining to our movement into the celestial world—are given to us.

The scriptures speak of the temple as "a house of learning" (D&C 88:119) and "a place of instruction" (D&C 97:13). By regularly participating in the temple ordinances and giving our complete attention to them, we begin to see how the whole thing is tied together and how God is training the minds and hearts of his children. He is educating us under the influence of the Holy Spirit and rewriting the scripts of our lives. If we properly prepare ourselves, we will receive a new wealth of knowledge every time we go.

A woman tells how she learned to receive personal revelation when attending the temple:

> For seventeen years I went to the temple believing that the only thing I was supposed to do was be the eyes and ears of the deceased people for whom I was doing the work. So I sat there with my eyes open so they could see

everything and my ears open so they could hear everything, and that was all I did for seventeen years.

Then I read an article about the temple being a house
of revelation, and that we were supposed to go there seeking revelation—that it was not only permissible, it was
what we were *supposed* to be doing. Well, what a revelation! And the floodgates opened.

I learned that I could go to the temple seeking personal revelation as well as looking for revelation about
what the ordinances mean. I take something personal to
the temple every time now—I never will go without a
question, without a concern, because I know it will be
answered. I will always, always walk away with the
impression of what I need to do. I know I'll get it.
Sometimes it comes in the car on the way there, sometimes it's on the way back, sometimes it will come a day
later, but if you go to the temple with your concern, I feel
like there's too much spirit there for it to be missed. You
just go there in prayer, often fasting, and those concerns
are addressed.

The Temple: A Model Home

Besides being a place of answers, the temple is also a model
home. It is "a house of glory, a house of order, a house of God"
(D&C 88:119). Christ is the model person, and his house is the
model home. Many people never had a model home. Go to the
temple and observe what happens there. Study it carefully—the
cleanliness, the order, the reverence, the divine purpose. We never
hear people raising their voices in the temple. Questions and
problems are handled with great respect and kindness. Everyone is
dressed equally; there is no emphasis on status or possessions;

everyone is God's own child. In the temple we experience a celestial culture.

Because of this, the temple can offer a healing experience to those who may have been wounded in other relationships. One woman described the feelings she had upon returning to the temple after her divorce was finalized:

> There was a short time when I wasn't able to have my temple recommend because I was going through a divorce. That was really, really hard for me because it was like being cut off from where I needed to be. I wanted to do everything I possibly could to get back. I felt, "What good is it to be a member of the Church if you can't have your temple recommend and be able to fulfill all the covenants you're supposed to do? What good is it to be baptized and be in the Church if you can't go all the way with it?" It's like almost living in vain without that.
>
> I remember when I was able to go back, I was so heartbroken and feeling downtrodden and alone. I had done all I could to regain my temple recommend, but I still felt like I had let my Father in Heaven down. I knew he loved me and cared about me and wanted me to be there, but inside I felt like I wasn't good enough. How could he forgive me for letting him down? I had decided to go through with the divorce, and I never really forgave myself totally, so I didn't think the Lord would forgive me. Of course, he would, but I still couldn't feel that way, and I felt all these burdens and heartaches.
>
> When I went back to the temple, it was almost like he put his arms around me and lifted all those burdens. I just can't explain how everything was lifted from me. I felt pure peace and the love of his arms around me.

All Six Transcendent Events Embodied in the Temple

I suggest that the temple embodies all six events of the Restoration. The first event, or the First Vision, has to do with identity and relationships. There is no other place on earth where our true identity and our relationship with Heavenly Father are so clearly defined as in the temple. The second event involves the divine mission of Jesus Christ, and this is the fundamental doctrine woven through every aspect of the temple ceremony. The third event relates to priesthood covenants, which are central to all temple ordinances. The fourth event has to do with the Church. In the temple, we agree to fully devote ourselves to the upbuilding of the Lord's latter-day church and kingdom. The fifth event involves the keys of salvation, and the temple is where we see the full manifestation of these keys in proclaiming the gospel, perfecting the Saints, and redeeming the dead. The sixth event, of course, is the restoration of the temple ordinances themselves.

The purest paradigms about every facet of life are presented in the temple. In fact, I suggest that every principle of the gospel—the whole plan of life and salvation—is taught in the temple, either by precept or by example. The more we go to the temple in the spirit of openness and preparation and prayer, the more we will find that it's a place of living revelation. I know that is true.

In the temple, the Lord can reaffirm in a powerful way our understanding of his plan for us, as one returned sister missionary discovered:

> When I came back from my mission, I was sure that the Lord was going to answer all my questions, and that because I had served a faithful mission, everything was just going to go boom, boom, boom, and fall into place. I was going to know exactly what to major in, and within

a year or so I was going to meet somebody who would fall madly in love with me because I was a good person and I was trying hard and I loved the Lord.

I just thought all these things were going to happen. But I had a really hard time getting into school, and was only admitted into night school, so I had a hard time getting into any of my classes. I was really hurt. I didn't understand why everything was such a struggle after I had just served a faithful mission. I was expecting to be blessed!

One day when all this was going on, I went to the temple with some of my friends. After the session, somebody came up and spoke to me. I had never seen her before and I have never seen her since, but she said something to me about how beautiful I looked, and that she could tell that I was really committed to the Lord, and that he loved me. At that moment something just clicked with me. My problems did not go away, but it was a moment of enlightenment. I walked out of the temple saying, "I can do this," and the answers to my prayers came, even though they didn't come when I wanted.

My life has gone very little like what I had planned for as a young woman. But I am not unhappy, and I am grateful that I can look back on that moment and change my attitude. That day in the temple has made all the difference for me. Most important, it affected my relationship with God, because I realized that he cares about me and that I'm not just down here by myself trying to figure everything out on my own.

Many vital principles like the truths experienced by that young woman are taught in the temple. We'll touch on just a few of them here.

Love

The word *love* is never mentioned in any outward way in the temple endowment, but it is taught in many, many ways. When we took our missionaries from Ireland to the London Temple, we discovered new ways of loving people that helped us become much more effective in sharing the gospel with them. We can love people by serving them and by teaching and testifying to them. But we also learned that we needed to pray for them and with them; to listen deeply to their hearts and understand them from the inside; to affirm them as God's own children; and to sacrifice for them.

The Prophet Joseph Smith said this about love: "Love is one of the chief characteristics of Deity, and ought to be manifested by those who aspire to be the sons of God. A man filled with the love of God is not content with blessing his family alone, but ranges through the whole world anxious to bless the whole human race" (*Teachings of the Prophet Joseph Smith,* 174). The Lord's love for us is made clear in the words of the prophet Isaiah: "Can a woman forget her sucking child, that she should not have compassion on the son of her womb? yea, they may forget, yet will I not forget thee. Behold, I have graven thee upon the palms of my hands" (Isaiah 49:15–16).

One of my dear missionaries, Elder Lloyd, passed away a number of years ago, and I was invited to attend his funeral service and to read his most cherished missionary experience. This is what he had written:

> We were teaching a widow lady, and we had gone through all of the discussions. She believed the gospel and she loved it, but she didn't act on it. As I thought about this, I realized that I hadn't loved her in all of the ways I had learned in the temple. I hadn't deeply affirmed her

and listened to her within her own frame of reference. So I decided to do that.

The next time we visited her home I said, "Sister, we've been doing a lot of teaching, but we would sure like to listen to you for a while."

She said, "Oh, elders, there's nothing to listen to. It's just something I have to deal with myself." I didn't say anything. "But I'll tell you one thing. My first husband, he tried to cram religion down my throat." Again I didn't say anything, and she continued. "He made me so mad that I don't know if I'm fully over it yet. It's not you, elders."

Then I said, "It sounds like you're really concerned about institutionalized religion; it's not so much us."

"Well, yes, I mean—I don't know . . ." Then she went on. She talked for maybe five or ten minutes at the most. Finally she said, "Elder Lloyd, never have I felt so understood by anyone as you. I would do anything you tell me to do."

I couldn't teach another word until I had sanctified myself. She was so ready, but I wasn't prepared. So my companion and I prepared ourselves, and then we came back and taught the same discussions in the same way. This time she accepted them and lived them. When we finished the discussions, she went into the waters of baptism, and all of her kids went with her.

After this experience, Elder Lloyd started bringing more people into the Church than entire districts, because he had learned in the temple how to truly love those whom he taught.

Another example of learning about love in the temple is shared by a mother who was struggling with a teenage son:

My son was going through this difficult period of time, and one day, in seminary, he was asked to pray at the end of the lesson. He has a rote prayer that he says every time—you know the type—and he prayed that the teacher would be blessed. And I thought, "That's me," because I was the teacher. But he never prays for his mom, never.

I went home and said to my husband, "I feel impressed to go to the temple. I need to go through the temple." So he took a day off work, and we went down to the temple. In the temple, I felt that physical blessing given in my son's prayer. I felt it go right through my body from head to toe—that his mom, his teacher, was blessed. And I was blessed with the feeling about my son, "He's in my hands; you don't need to worry."

That is what the temple does to me. When I've done everything I can do, I go there, and the Lord says, "My turn. Don't worry. This is beyond your capabilities." To know that my son is watched over like that brings a peace to me as a parent that can come in no other way.

Prayer

While I was serving as mission president in Ireland, the mission supervisor, Elder Mark E. Petersen of the Quorum of the Twelve, invited the mission presidents of the West European Mission to the London Temple for a special prayer circle to be directed by President Henry D. Moyle of the First Presidency in behalf of the Church's efforts to obtain a tax-free status for the London Temple. We had lost in the lower court and also in the courts of appeal, and the case eventually went to the supreme court of the land, which is the House of Lords. President Moyle had been assigned by the First Presidency to work on this case and follow up. My own grandfather, Stephen L Richards, who was President David O. McKay's first counselor, had also worked on the case prior to his passing away and had prepared a brief that could be read in the court dealing with the essence of what takes place in the temple. The brief was used in each appeal. Our solicitors, as attorneys are called in England, were nonmembers, and this was all part of their preparation.

President Moyle was the mouth in this special prayer, and in the prayer he said that the main purpose of this whole legal endeavor was to have the gospel taught in the House of Lords, to have a testimony borne even through the mouth of a non-LDS solicitor of the restoration of the gospel and the importance of the temple for sacred ceremonies for the living and the dead. He prophetically asked the Lord to inspire our solicitor with words and powers beyond his natural capacity and to frustrate the opposing counsel with an inability to effectively put forth their case and not to know why.

I'm a personal witness to the fulfillment of those prophetic statements. (The mission presidents were invited as guests to sit in the outside fringe of the House of Lords as the presentations were made.) The Spirit was strong in that room of the House of Lords, and the prophecies given in the prayer were literally fulfilled. The opposing solicitor was frustrated and unable to frame his arguments and his words as he desired, and he acknowledged that he could not and also acknowledged that he didn't know why he could not. Our solicitor was empowered beyond his natural capacity, made a brilliant and persuasive presentation, and essentially gave a testimony of our church in the House of Lords. It was one of the most memorable, inspiring things I have ever witnessed. It is my understanding that we lost the case but that the temple was not taxed. I don't understand the full spiritual significance of what happened that day—it may have been a necessary step in the prospering of the Church in that beautiful country. But I will never forget the power of that prayer.

In the temple we learn how to pray in a perfect way, and this gives us a model to follow as we prepare for our daily prayers. It reminds us to resolve any ill feelings we might have toward other people. "Go thy way unto thy brother, and first be reconciled to thy brother, and then come unto me with full purpose of heart, and I will receive you" (3 Nephi 12:24). It reminds us to think deeply about each of our covenants with the Lord and to come back to the gospel path if we have strayed in any way. The Lord has said, "Thy vows shall be offered up in righteousness on all days and at all times" (D&C 59:11). It also reminds us that prayer should be more than a quick monologue or a checklist of needs and wants. We need to keep our hearts open and influenceable so that we can enjoy a two-way communication with our Heavenly Father.

Walking into the Presence of God

In the temple we see ourselves symbolically walk into the presence of God. Why does the Lord want us to have that experience? He's trying to give us an awareness of who we are and what we can become. The world doesn't teach that at all; it teaches entirely different kinds of goals. And we can get so immersed in the world that we forget our true identity and destination. If we will simply stay in the gospel covenant, we will go to the celestial kingdom. In the temple, we literally see ourselves doing that.

I believe this experience is profoundly important, especially for people who have never been treated that way—people who have been put down and compared and judged and categorized until they have begun to believe that the image in the social mirror is who they really are. The evil one, whose main tool is discouragement, tells us that we can't do it, that we're not spiritually minded, that we're not celestial material, and so forth. But the Lord's program is designed to overcome those false and negative images. In the gospel, and especially in the temple, everything is geared to the unleashing of our divine potential.

I pray that our Heavenly Father will help us to truly make the temple the center of our worship. And as we fully prepare ourselves and learn to concentrate on the things of eternity, I pray that we will receive the fullness of the Holy Ghost that dwells in the house of the Lord.

Internalizing the Sixth Event

Recognizing that the whole purpose for the temple is the creation of eternal, intergenerational families, I have suggested as basic initiatives some of the foundational principles our prophets have given us for building strong families. Temple worship itself has little point if we are not attending to our primary family responsibilities.

Once we have set our own houses in order, we are in a better position to reach out to our extended family members. The service initiative for this event invites us to consider ways to strengthen our families through all their generations, acting as "transition figures" if necessary to put an end to cyclical transgressions where they exist.

First, there is the process of connecting with the Father and the Son through prayer or with another person through deep listening, affirming, and serving. This is followed by the process of justification, or becoming perfect *in* Christ through ordinances. And then there is the lifelong process of sanctification—receiving more and more of the influence of the Holy Ghost in perfecting one's motives, actions, words, and thoughts—becoming perfect *like* Christ.

The second theme is the connection with the Father in the First Vision, the Son through the Atonement, and the role of the Holy Ghost in all of the other events, so that more and more of his gifts and powers are impregnated into our natures.

Third, you will notice that the six events begin with ideas, correct concepts, doctrine, or paradigms about identity, relationships, and the gospel. Then those ideas are given structure through priesthood and the Church organization. This leads to behavior, areas for action, for doing, for building a strong, celestial family.

Finally, you'll notice in the first two events that we *receive* knowledge of God, our role, and the power of the Atonement. In the next two we learn to *give* through priesthood and church work. In the last two, we *create*. We make the Church's three purposes happen, and we create a family, new children in the context of an extended, intergenerational family.

Themes of the Six Events

Connection	Justification (perfect *in* Christ)	Sanctification (perfect *like* Christ)
Father	Son	Holy Ghost
Ideas, Identity, Relationships	Structure	Behavior
Receive	Give	Create

Basic Level— Personal Initiatives	Advanced Level— Enlarging Service Initiatives
1. Offer daily, listening prayers of faith.	1. Build strong human relationships through profound listening, affirming, and caring service.
2. Ponder the scriptures daily to feast on the words and love of Jesus Christ. ("Give us this day our daily bread.")	2. Teach and testify, by the Spirit, of Christ and his atoning sacrifice.
3. Exercise "repentance unto baptism," or partake of the sacrament worthily (obeying "general commandments—becoming perfect *in* Christ").	3. Forgive all others and rebuild wounded relationships, as guided by the Spirit (obeying "personal commandments").
4. Magnify priesthood and Church callings.	4. Magnify "outside-the-Church" callings as given by the Spirit.
5. Give honest, diligent service in prayerfully seeking referrals, attending to "temporal" matters, and worshipping in the temple.	5. Seeing all things as stewardship, "bend your whole soul" in righteous living, in establishing Zion (becoming perfect *like* Christ).
6. Hold daily family prayer, weekly family home evenings, and consistent, scripture-centered devotionals.	**6. Build a gospel-centered intergenerational family, including the work of "transition figures."**

PART 3

THE PERSONAL
RESTORATION

THE SIGNIFICANCE
OF THE SEQUENCE

THE SIGNIFICANCE
OF THE SEQUENCE

I N THIS BOOK WE HAVE EXAMINED the six transcendent events of the Restoration as the model God uses to save and exalt his children. But in reality there is a *seventh* event: the restoration of the gospel to each of us on a deeply personal level. In a sense, this is the most significant event of all. Without it, the entire model is nothing but an intellectual exercise, and thus it can never really make a difference in our individual lives. But when this personal restoration takes place, it gives us a new birth, one so real and penetrating that it profoundly affects our thoughts and feelings and behavior.

How can the gospel be restored to us personally? How can it be restored to our children and to other people we care about? The word *restoration* means a bringing back of something we had before, and we all had a knowledge of the gospel of Jesus Christ before we came to earth. How is this knowledge restored to us in mortality?

President Joseph F. Smith once asked, "Can we know anything here that we did not know before we came?" He said that "all those salient truths which come home so forcibly to the head and heart seem but the awakening of the memories of the spirit. . . . In coming here, we forgot all, that our agency might be free indeed, to choose good or evil, that we might merit the reward of our own choice and conduct. But *by the power of the Spirit,* . . . we often catch a spark from the awakened memories of the immortal soul, which lights up our whole being as with the glory of our former home" (*Gospel Doctrine,* 13–14; emphasis added).

Thus the gospel truly can be restored to each of us, but it must come through the instrumentality of the Holy Ghost. "The things of God knoweth no man, except he has the Spirit of God" (JST 1 Corinthians 2:11). It's not enough to have membership in the Church or to study its doctrines; we must experience a personal restoration "by the power of the Spirit." Until this happens, we may think of religion and life as being in two separate compartments. We may be *active* in the Church but *inactive* in the gospel. And we may wonder why we don't have the regenerating sense of security and moral courage that others seem to have.

I believe that missionary work is a nearly perfect metaphor for understanding how to have the six events of the Restoration restored to each one of us. In missionary work, people primarily experience the first event simply in the way the missionaries treat them—they treat them as if they were God's own children, which of course they are. The missionaries give them love when they may not have deserved it. In short, they build identity and a relationship and begin to testify of God, of Christ, and of who the people really are. The second event takes place as the people start to study the gospel to understand how the whole plan of life and salvation revolves around Jesus Christ and his atoning sacrifice, which has to be received by faith and repentance. Then comes the third event of receiving priesthood ordinances, by baptism and the gift of the

Holy Ghost, and then the fourth event, by entrance into God's church. The people gradually become more and more service-oriented within the Church, and also missionary-oriented outside the Church, and also temple-oriented to reach their dead ancestry, and also family-oriented in looking to have all of their temple blessings and sealings for their own family, and then for their inter-generational family, and then for the extended family, until eventually it embodies the family of God, the whole human race.

Once they receive the fullness of the Holy Ghost, which is manifested most completely in the temple, they have consecrated themselves to God's holy purposes. Then they interpret everything as a stewardship, including children, jobs, possessions, vacations, and everything else. Consecration precedes stewardship. The same process is true in doing home teaching and visiting teaching and reactivation work and, when understood through the divine cultural lens, everything we do in the Church and in our lives. So the question becomes, how do we ourselves come to these six events of the Restoration? The answer is simply to help other people come to them. It is a clear illustration of the Savior's teaching that only when we lose our life for his sake can we find it. To find our true identity, we find Christ. We covenant. We become actively involved in his Church. We work on the three purposes of the Church. And we build an intergenerational family that can bear the weight of eternity.

Honoring the Sequence of the Six Events

Constant effort is required if we want to have the gospel restored to us individually. I suggest that many people fail to have this experience—and to help others do so—because they make one or more of the following mistakes: (1) they violate the sequence of the events; (2) they focus on only one or two or a few events but not all six; or (3) they forget that once the gospel has been fully restored to a person, the process must be continually renewed.

Thus the first key to experiencing the personal restoration is to *honor the sequence* of the six transcendent events. Let's quickly review that sequence and the important questions answered by those events:

1. The First Vision: "Who is God, and who am I?"
2. The restoration of the gospel through the Book of Mormon: "Whose am I?"
3. The restoration of the priesthood: "How can I receive Christ?"
4. The restoration of the Church: "Where do I go to receive Christ?"
5. The restoration of the keys of salvation for the living and the dead: "What is the work I should do in life?"
6. The restoration of the temple ordinances: "Why did God bring about the Restoration?"

As I said in the introductory section, the "*when*" question is answered by the *sequence* of these six events. I believe this is truly the heart of the Lord's problem-solving model, and I think the biggest mistake we make in parenting, teaching, leading, and building relationships is that we don't honor the sequence he established in this model. In my view, knowing *when* to do *what* is the essence of wisdom.

In bringing the world out of a state of apostasy, God gave us a perfect pattern to use in working with our family members and other people. How did he do it? Notice that he revealed light and knowledge in a particular order: first he dealt with *identity and relationships;* then *concepts* (that is, the gospel); then *structure or organization* (that is, the ordinances and the Church); and finally *actions or behavior.* That's very important. If we want to help our children or other people change their behavior, we begin by improving the quality of our *relationships* with them. And we introduce new *ideas* before we introduce new expectations and controls. In other words, we help them see the world differently. When a person's paradigm changes, everything else changes with it.

The Lord's model teaches us that conceptual interventions should always precede structural interventions, and this pattern applies to everything we do in life. In my professional field of organizational development, I'm deeply interested in change. How do we change an organization or a culture? How do we change a person? The best way to find out is to study how God does it, because he is the master of change. How does he bring about change among his children? As we examine what he does, we see that everything takes place "line upon line"; there is no quick, easy shortcut. So if we want to help business or professional organizations become more effective, for example, we must change the way people *think* before we change their structures and systems. By laying a solid foundation and then building on it one step at a time, we can eventually arrive at partnership agreements that provide a clear, mutual understanding of what is expected.

This concept of sequence is one of the most important things I've learned in my personal and professional work. As Joseph Smith put it, "It is necessary for us to have an understanding of God himself in the beginning. If we start right, it is easy to go right all the time; but if we start wrong we may go wrong, and it will be a hard matter to get right" (*History of the Church*, 6:302).

To use the Lord's problem-solving model effectively, we must honor the sequence. I often ask audiences, "How many of you crammed in school? How many got good at it? How many of you have worked on a farm? Have you ever crammed on the farm?" If a farmer forgets to plant in the spring and plays all summer, it doesn't matter how hard he works during the harvest season—he won't have a crop.

The same thing can happen when we work with people. We try to get them to the temple before they are truly matured in the Church. We try to reactivate them in the Church before they really understand the covenants and the gospel. Or we try to get them into the gospel before they know who they are and have a sense of being loved. We get impatient and violate the sequence.

What happens if we try to get people into the second event (the gospel) before they understand their identity and trust their relationship with us? They won't be open to it. What happens if we try to get people into the fourth event (the Church) before they've experienced the first three? They may be baptized, but they will blow away with the first storm. To have staying power, they must be *converted.*

Far too often, people get into the Church without ever getting deeply into the gospel. Thus they become active in the Church but remain inactive in the gospel. That is, they don't continually go back to the covenant process so that they can be nurtured in the Savior's love through the power of his atoning sacrifice. As a result, they eventually start losing the spiritual food within and become subject to the environment around them. If that environment is positive and uplifting, they do well. But if it tests them—if they have to deal with members and leaders who are human and therefore make mistakes—they get offended and begin to withdraw. They are like the seeds that "fell upon stony places, where they had not much earth: . . . and when the sun was up, they were scorched; and because they had no root, they withered away" (Matthew 13:5–6).

Once members of the Church begin to withdraw from fellowship, they often get into a cycle of looking for evidence to justify their withdrawal—and they inevitably find it, because all people are imperfect. In the process, they also withdraw from the real source of their spiritual sustenance and power. In some cases they turn to other sources; for instance, they may associate with groups that are critical of the Church or start reading anti-Mormon literature (which is like pornography to the soul). Thus the seeds of doubt multiply and grow, causing them to become cynical and critical and eventually to leave the path entirely. They may even go back to apostate notions of salvation, losing the whole concept of becoming perfect *in* Christ through constant renewal of the gospel covenant.

My wife and I know a couple who once joined the Church primarily because of the social nurturing they received from other Latter-day Saints. When they were sealed in the temple, many of us traveled a great distance to be there and show our love and support. The couple felt very happy and fulfilled, and they became deeply involved in various callings in the Church. For example, the woman was an unusually competent organizer and leader, and she managed the visiting teaching program better than it had ever been done before. After a while new Relief Society leaders were called, and this sister was given a different assignment. A less competent woman took charge of the visiting teaching program, and it began to suffer as a result.

By that time, the "honeymoon" period had also passed in the couple's social relationships with other ward members. They were part of the team, but they were now expected to give as well as receive. A new bishopric came in with a different style and different approaches that were very upsetting to the couple. After a number of unhappy experiences, they gradually became disenchanted and disaffected. Eventually they developed a spirit of criticism and faultfinding toward the Church.

During our mission in Ireland, I saw an entire branch built in Belfast on the personal power of two dynamic missionaries who were filled with love and with the Spirit. Because the new converts were so deeply dependent on these elders, they were easily uprooted as they came to the rickety old building where the branch met and discovered the weaknesses of the other members. The branch was built up in just a few months, and it was practically destroyed in about the same period of time as soon as the missionaries were gone. The problem was that these people had gone straight into the fourth event of the Restoration (Church) without ever experiencing the earlier events. They had come into the Church without really receiving the gospel, and they had never understood the concept of entering into a covenant with Christ and renewing it every week at the sacrament table.

The same thing can happen when Church members go to the temple before they're really prepared. I had a good friend who was a very powerful teacher of temple preparation seminars. The sheer strength of his personality and the tremendous love he expressed kept people coming to his classes, but they never truly understood Christ and the gospel. In a sense, they became hero-worshipers who focused on a human being rather than on the Savior. As each seminar ended and a new group replaced the old one, the "graduates" lost their base of support. They went to the temple, but many went ill prepared, and within a week or two they removed their temple garments. They were built on a sandy foundation, not on the foundation of Christ.

The Book of Mormon identifies the true foundation that will anchor us in the Church and the gospel: "Remember, remember that it is upon the rock of our Redeemer, who is Christ, the Son of God, that ye must build your foundation; that when the devil shall send forth his mighty winds, yea, his shafts in the whirlwind, yea, when all his hail and his mighty storm shall beat upon you, it shall have no power over you to drag you down to the gulf of misery and endless wo, because of the rock upon which ye are built, which is a sure foundation, a foundation whereon if men build they cannot fall" (Helaman 5:12).

Understanding Sequences

Once we understand the significance of sequence in the Lord's work, we can look at a variety of things in a whole new light. Consider, for example, the Articles of Faith. Articles 1 through 3 deal with God, man, and Christ, discussing essentially the concerns of the first two events of the Restoration. Article 4 enumerates basic principles and ordinances of the gospel, Articles 5 and 6 go more deeply into Church organization, and so forth.

Here are some additional examples of sequencing that are worth considering:

- The Lord's commission to Moses (see Moses, chapter 1)
- The Savior's teachings to the Nephites at the temple in Bountiful (see 3 Nephi 11–20)
- The temple endowment ceremony
- The process of finding and teaching investigators and re-activating members
- Priesthood and auxiliary work

Helping Others Experience a Personal Restoration

President Ezra Taft Benson said, "The Lord works from the inside out. The world works from the outside in. . . . The world would mold men by changing their environment. Christ changes men, who then change their environment. The world would shape human behavior, but Christ can change human nature" (*The Teachings of Ezra Taft Benson,* 79). Thus the process by which people are converted involves a particular sequence of events.

When babies are born, they immediately begin to form a sense of their own identity through their relationships with parents and other loved ones. That's like the first event. And if children don't bond with their parents in their early years, it's far more difficult for the parents to reach them later on, because the children haven't developed a sense of their own worth. Thus we should often communicate with our children in ways that basically tell them, "You can succeed. You're a capable person. Ignore the social mirror, because you're a celestial candidate." And then we should treat them accordingly until they deeply believe these things. The key in building a celestial family is how you treat the one who tests you the most. If you can show unconditional love to that one, the other children really know that they are unconditionally loved as well.

Even in our Primary classes, we usually teach little children that Christ is their friend and their model before we teach them that he is their Savior. We teach them about Heavenly Father and Jesus, and we build a loving relationship with them. It is critically important that people grow up in an atmosphere of being affirmed as God's own children—not as his creations, but as spirit children who are literally one generation away from our Eternal Father.

As missionaries, we do the same thing in working with investigators. We don't go in and immediately try to get them into the Church. We don't even teach them about Christ at the very beginning. Before we do anything else, we treat them as if they *were* Christ. We love them and their children even more than they do, because we know who they really are. That's what charity is—the pure love of Christ, which is the Father's love. In a sense, we see them as a father would see them. And this love enables us to be strong with them and to help them discipline themselves to live the standards of the gospel and prepare for the ordinance of baptism.

Whenever we're trying to bring people closer to the Savior, we must be as Christlike as possible. Before we can help them accept Christ as their model, we must first be models ourselves and build strong relationships with them. We must reflect the Savior's perfect love for them. If we're conditional in our love and we're essentially manipulating people in order to rush them into the gospel or the Church, we've violated the sequence. We can't even teach them about the Atonement until they feel our love and a true sense of worth in their relationship with us. They have to feel that very deeply. Otherwise they may perceive that we view them as statistics, and that is devastating to people. The personal restoration is a *process,* and it must unfold in the way the Lord has established.

But it takes tremendous patience and self-restraint not to rush in too soon with our gospel answers. These answers may be true, but we can hurt and condemn people by giving them truth before they are ready for it. We must let the Spirit guide us, and we must be very patient.

This process can sometimes take years. It's like planting a certain species of Chinese bamboo tree—we see nothing for four years except a little shoot, because all of the growth is underground. But if we diligently nurture the plant during those first four years, in the fifth year it will grow up to eighty feet high! Likewise, by patiently following the Restoration pattern as we lead people to the Savior, we are helping them sink deep roots that will eventually drive them to grow "unto the measure of the stature of the fulness of Christ" (Ephesians 4:13).

Jumping Ahead Too Quickly

While I was serving as a mission president in Ireland, I became alerted by the missionaries that they were teaching the son of a prominent judge. They were trying to get the permission of this boy's parents for him to be baptized. His mother deferred to the judgment of his father, and his father was a person of great spirituality with a knowledge of the scriptures, a person of social and political importance, and a person of great intellect and deep integrity. So he said before he would give permission to his son, he would need to understand what his son was getting into.

The missionaries involved me in helping to teach Judge McCracken. Because of his integrity, his openness of heart and mind, his faith in Jesus Christ, and his prayerfulness, he came to understand and believe the restored gospel. He had to deal with the heavy tradition and the social pressures and political consequences of his decision, but he was a strong person and feared God more than man. He gave permission for his son to be baptized, and shortly thereafter he was baptized. He seemed to be "called out of due season" as Paul was, because no one around him understood how he could possibly do such a thing.

The judge belonged to a religious study group that had studied the Bible for many years, and he invited me to come to his home to speak to this group. This is the way he introduced me: "All of you know that I have become a Mormon, that I have joined The Church of Jesus Christ of Latter-day Saints. All of you think I have made the most serious mistake of my life, and you have no way of understanding how I could possibly do such a foolish thing. We all care for each other, and you know that I am not a person who would make such a decision lightly, in that I have the courage of my convictions. We have all for years wondered about the return of Elijah as prophesied in Malachi. I want to testify to you that Elijah has returned to the earth and restored his keys and powers. This gentleman is a missionary who has come from his home in America to teach us about the return of Elijah." That was the introduction he gave to my presentation—totally out of the blue. But these were people of great intellectual integrity and spirituality who knew that the prophecies about Elijah were to come to pass. They also knew somewhat about Elijah's mission dealing with families. They were open and responsive, but none of them opted to go further in understanding the other events of the Restoration.

I have since wondered, though, if perhaps one of the problems in the approach we took was that we didn't go through the proper sequence but rather jumped to the fifth event before the foundation had been laid. I think that Judge McCracken was operating on the belief that the group would be open to knowing about the return of Elijah because they had been praying for it, preparing for it, and believing in it, and that this would be an opening that would create the opportunity to teach the whole story of the Restoration. This was a valuable experience that may at some time open doors for those righteous souls to understand the gospel, but the true significance of Elijah's return cannot really be understood outside the context of the earlier events of the Restoration.

Why Do We Violate the Sequence?

Sometimes the reason we violate the sequence of the divine pattern is that it's not fully operational in *our own* lives. For instance, parents who are focused on their public image will have a hard time feeling unconditional love toward a child who takes the wrong path. They will essentially try to manipulate him or her in some way, because they really don't have "an eye single to the glory of God" (D&C 4:5). Their main goal is not to bring about God's purpose, which is the growth and development of the child, but rather to get recognition from other people. Why? Because their social software tells them that they must rely on people's perceptions of them for their own sense of worth and security.

Our capacity to help others depends on *our own* experience with all six events in the Lord's model. Unless the gospel is continually restored to us, we won't remain centered in Christ. We'll tend to become impatient, anxious, overreactive, and critical—even toward the people we love. And then we'll throw *them* out of sequence, thus compounding and enlarging their problems rather than moving them toward a solution.

One of our missionaries in Ireland had spent most of his life in foster homes. He was on a mission because of social pressure, and he came with a chip on his shoulder that affected all of his relationships. He resisted the mission rules and fought his companion. "I'm not going to turn weird and become this holy Joe," he said. "I'm not as spiritual as everybody else, and I'm not going to change."

One day my wife, Sandra, was talking with this elder in the mission home. (She often held informal "interviews" with the missionaries right in the hallway, and many of them opened up far more with her than they ever did with me.) He told her that he had lived in about twelve foster homes and had been pushed around and beat up so much that it was hard for him to trust people. In fact, he didn't really know what it was like to be loved. He could remember only one brief summer when a mother in a foster home had treated him with love and kindness. He shared this experience with Sandra and then told her, "I feel this with you and your husband." In a sense, that was the first event for him.

We patiently worked with him over a period of time, and he gradually overcame his worldly attitudes and started getting into the gospel. As he came to feel God's love, he was no longer dependent on the treatment he received from other people. He had tapped into the ultimate source of security, so he could say, "I've now learned how to love." His personal experience with the second event allowed him to extend the Savior's love, which he felt more fully, to others. After that he covenanted and committed himself to the Church and to his missionary work, and he continued to grow and develop toward spiritual maturity. Following an honorable mission, he married a young woman in the temple and pursued a course that would enable him to continually experience all of the events in the Restoration model.

If I wanted to help restore these six events to a family member or someone else who was lost, I wouldn't necessarily talk about the Church or the gospel at first. I would start by building a relationship with him. If he were open at all, I would try to get him to share his concerns and self-doubts in an atmosphere that would assure him he would not be judged. I would listen to him so deeply and empathetically that I could really get inside his agenda and understand his mind and heart from his own frame of reference.

I would affirm him as a child of God, a person of infinite worth who is precious to our Heavenly Father. I would get my heart close to his heart, and I would serve him—even sacrifice for him—in a way that would show him I truly love him and believe in him. I would pray for him and let him know that I'm doing so. If he would let me, I would also pray *with* him. I would testify of the Father's love for him. Little by little, I would try to help him discover his identity and his relationship with God.

At the right moment, I would tell him what Christ and the Atonement mean to me. I would express my love for the Savior in such a way that he could sense the sincerity and the depth of that love. I would tell him that I'm not an ideal person but that I am trying to change and become better. If he became centered on me, he would lose faith as he discovered my weaknesses, so I would try to get him centered on Christ, who is perfect.

As the Spirit began to work on him, he might ask me how he could get closer to the Lord. I would explain that we do that through the ordinances and covenants of the priesthood. I would teach him how the sacrament renews us and how the Holy Ghost works, describing these blessings in such a way that he would want to be worthy of them. Working with his priesthood leaders, I would gradually try to get him involved in some responsibility in the Church—perhaps a very small one at first. After he began to mature in his experience in the Church, I would help him prepare to go to the temple, where the eternal family is created, and to fulfill his role in that eternal family.

Through the six transcendent events of the Restoration, the Lord has made the gospel available to the entire human family. And in doing so, he has given us a divine pattern to use in our own lives and in our roles as parents, teachers, missionaries, leaders, and friends. It's a perfect system for restoring the gospel to all of our Heavenly Father's children, because we all knew these truths before we were born. And this should be very encouraging to us as we work to help our family members and others regain the light and knowledge they once had.

THE IMPORTANCE
OF EXPERIENCING
ALL SIX EVENTS

THE IMPORTANCE
OF EXPERIENCING
ALL SIX EVENTS

T HE SECOND KEY TO THE PERSONAL restoration is to make sure that we *experience all six events* in the Lord's model, because it's not sufficient to focus on only one or two or even five of them. For instance, although it's vital that we learn to love other people, that alone will not bring us to Christ and his kingdom.

When I was called to serve as a mission president, I learned that only about one-third of the members in Ireland were active in the Church. We were very concerned about the many people who had fallen away. They had once received the gospel by covenant, but the old software had moved in and they had left the eternal path. In many cases they had transferred responsibility to the missionaries or to the Church, expecting others to take care of them and nurture them. They were unaware that they were fundamentally responsible to work out their own salvation.

We wanted to help restore the gospel to these people. They had already been visited by others who had tried to get them back into the Church. But they had never really experienced a renewal of the first event, so they didn't have a true sense of their worth and identity in those relationships.

I've sometimes said to audiences, "If the air were taken out of this room right now, you would all lose interest in what I'm talking about—you'd all leave instantly. Does air motivate you? No. It's the *absence* of air that motivates you. But now that you have air, you're excited about learning." And then I've asked, "Do you know what the emotional or psychological equivalent of air is? It's feeling understood." In other words, it's central in the first event.

So what did we do with the less-active members in Ireland? We gave them emotional air. For three months, we assigned four sets of missionaries to do nothing but visit them and begin the process of restoring the gospel to them. However, we had to give the missionaries a little training first, because they were eager to rush in with gospel answers and quick scriptural formulas about what these people should do. We told the missionaries not to focus on getting them back into the Church but rather to listen deeply and just build relationships—to give them air and let them live with this air until their natural inclinations developed. Once people have air, they become open and want to learn. We said, "Just go visit with them and listen to them. You have two ears and one mouth; use them accordingly. Listen with your heart, and listen to the Spirit. At the end of the visit, you might remind them when meetings are held, but don't apply any pressure at all. They must feel that you love them regardless of their decisions, and that your only goal is to understand them."

Thus the missionaries, literally God's mortal angels, visited these people and responded to their deep hungers and needs. They had never been listened to with such intensity or felt so much human affirmation, and they truly opened up. What was the result? Within two weeks, almost half of the people the missionaries visited came back! A month later, however, nearly two-thirds of that group had fallen away again. Why? Because they didn't experience the other five events. We tried to help bring that about, but only people who are deeply converted to Christ and his Atonement can have the gospel fully restored to them. There are many who never reach that point.

Here's another illustration of focusing on only one event. One of the elders in our mission was a true extremist. He fasted all of the time for this person or that person. At the same time, he had a companion who was slothful and unspiritual—it was like a companionship between a publican and a Pharisee.

In one of my interviews with this elder, I reminded him that the General Authorities had counseled us not to fast too often. I told him that he should fast once a month with the Saints and that he might occasionally have a special fast when the Spirit moved upon him to do so. But he replied that the Spirit was moving on him all of the time.

I said, "You've heard Elder Mark E. Petersen himself counsel us against this."

"Well," he responded, "who should I follow—you or God?" I asked him if he thought there was a difference between what his priesthood leaders were telling him and what the Lord was telling him, and he answered yes.

Then I told him, "Elder, you have the right to receive a confirmation of what you're being taught, but let me share with you what I think is happening. You're escaping from the challenge of dealing with a companion who doesn't have the background you have in the scriptures and so forth. You're focusing on your vertical relationship with the Lord, but he wants you to focus on this horizontal relationship. In fact, you can't really do the Lord's work unless you work on the horizontal relationship, because his whole purpose is to endow you with the power to bless other people, including your companion. If you don't learn to do that, you may fall into the trap that many missionaries do: you may become a social catalyst to help people come into the Church, but you won't develop the power to truly reach their hearts. The private victory is the key to the public victory."

He said, "Boy, that's so true. I've never learned to love other people—I don't know how." In other words, he responded with the beginning of a broken heart and a contrite spirit. As a result, he was able to get back on the path and to start becoming a more effective missionary.

But those who don't win the private victories can be easily disturbed and uprooted when they encounter the public challenges of life. They may find fault with the Church, or they may become unbalanced by focusing exclusively on one aspect of its mission. President Boyd K. Packer once noted the danger of such an imbalance:

> The gospel might be likened to the keyboard of a piano—a full keyboard with a selection of keys on which one who is trained can play a variety of music without limits. . . .
>
> How shortsighted it is, then, to choose a single key and endlessly tap out the monotony of a single note, or even two or three notes, when the full keyboard of limitless harmony can be played.
>
> How disappointing when the fullness of the gospel, the whole keyboard, is here upon the earth, that many . . . tap on a single key. The note they stress may be essential to a complete harmony of religious experience, but it is, nonetheless, not all there is. It isn't the fullness. . . .
>
> Some members of the Church who should know

better pick out a hobby key or two and tap them incessantly, to the irritation of those around them. They can dull their own spiritual sensitivities. They lose track that there is a fullness of the gospel. . . . They may reject the fullness in preference to a favorite note. This becomes exaggerated and distorted, leading them away into apostasy ("The Only True and Living Church," *Ensign,* December 1971, 41–42).

An example of this problem would be a tendency to focus on missionary work to the exclusion of family history and temple work, or a tendency to focus on the spiritual side of perfecting the Saints without emphasizing the temporal side, or vice versa. This kind of imbalance causes people to become seduced, as it were, by another center, another pair of glasses from which they get their identity and security. Their power comes from another source, not from Christ.

As we work to experience our personal restoration and to bring others to this knowledge, let us keep in mind not only the sequence of the six events but also the importance of *each* one of them in the whole model.

A CONSTANT
RENEWAL

CHAPTER 12

A CONSTANT
RENEWAL

AFTER ALL OF THE SIX EVENTS HAVE BEEN restored to us, we must pay the price to *constantly renew the process* so that we can experience this personal restoration every day. President Ezra Taft Benson taught that "the spirit, as well as the body, is in need of constant nourishment. Yesterday's meal is not enough to sustain today's needs" (*The Teachings of Ezra Taft Benson*, 60).

I believe that we need to experience *all* six events of the Restoration in our personal lives daily, or at least weekly. This takes constant effort, but it becomes a powerful source of renewal, growth, and direction as we progress along the path to eternal life. When we truly prepare ourselves, these six events are restored to us each time we go to the temple, every week when we partake of the sacrament, and continuously as we engage in meaningful, fervent prayer.

The key is to never move away from your own "sacred grove," the richness of your *own* private prayers. The Lord will give you a sense of what is appropriate for you to say and to commit yourself to each day. Spend time meditating on your true identity and what it says about your worth and potential, and thank your Heavenly

Father for revealing the knowledge of who you really are. Spend time focusing on the Savior; try to visualize his suffering and death, and express your deep gratitude for his infinite atonement. Reflect on the sacred covenants you have made with the Lord. Thank him for the ordinances of the priesthood and the gift of the Holy Ghost. If you have been endowed in the temple, slowly review each covenant in your mind and consider how it should affect your priorities and decisions during this period of your life.

Next, reflect on your membership in the Church—and in your family, since families are the foundation of the Church. Think about your callings in the Church, and ask yourself whether you're truly magnifying those callings. Ponder on the threefold mission of the Church—proclaiming the gospel, perfecting the Saints, and redeeming the dead—and review your own opportunities and efforts to help carry out those purposes. Spend time meditating on your stewardship in your home. Consider each family member by name, and let the Lord tell you by his Spirit what he wants you to know and do about them. And expand the reach of your prayer at times to include members of your extended family.

Don't be in too big a hurry to get off your knees. Your purpose is to be changed, to have a broken heart and a contrite spirit, to feel a sense of being commissioned to accomplish the Lord's purposes that day. All six events are restored to you through such a prayer, and you can rise up and bless everyone around you.

The spiritual nourishment we need comes from returning each day to our own "sacred grove," as it were. We must go to our Heavenly Father in prayer and deeply commit ourselves to obey his commandments. We must study and ponder the scriptures, especially the Book of Mormon. We must let the Spirit of God distill upon us as the dews from heaven. And one day we will arise and start to discover that we're no longer dependent on other people for our sense of identity and security, because it comes from a higher source. Then we can love others as the Lord does, even those who don't return our love.

Private Victories Lead to Public Victories

The key to this renewal process is the daily private victory. When a person visualizes his day and wins a private victory before the day even begins, and when he consistently stays within that frame of reference and lives according to his vision, he becomes an unending source of blessings to everybody.

In other words, the private victory leads to the public victory. The spiritual creation precedes the physical creation. Gethsemane precedes Calvary. And the same sequence is found in the Restoration model: the private victory is achieved in the first three events, the public victory in the last three. As we reestablish our relationship with our Heavenly Father, recenter ourselves in Christ, and recommit ourselves to the gospel covenants, we are preparing ourselves to accomplish our Church duties—especially those that pertain to our eternal families. (And those duties include the family welfare farm, or our employment.) When we do all these things under the guidance of the Spirit, we are building Zion. That is the public victory.

Furthermore, the key to the private victory is the public challenge. To achieve the private victory, we need the demands of a public challenge that transcends our own natural capacity. Where do we find such a challenge? We find it every day in the work of the Church, and particularly in marriage and family life, which is the most exacting and demanding challenge of all because it's so intimate and so constant. If we weren't thrown out of our comfort zone by the requirement to serve other people, our efforts to draw closer to God would be a kind of fabricated spirituality. Like the missionary who was fasting all of the time, we would be living in an artificial world, focusing only on the vertical relationship and ignoring the horizontal.

It's also important to understand where the private victory is won. In a sense, we all live three lives. The first is a *public* life, when we're around other people and sensitive to how they're perceiving us. The second is a *private* life, when we're either alone or with a loved one or close friend and just being ourselves. The third is what we might call a *secret* life or a deep inner life. Many people seldom enter this secret life. It's a level of self-awareness that allows us to stand apart from our private and public lives and observe our involvement in them. The apostle Paul said, "Let a man examine himself" (1 Corinthians 11:28), and that's what this secret life enables us to do. For example, we can examine our mental or emotional state by asking ourselves, *What kind of mood am I in right now? Are my motives totally in alignment with my covenants? Is the Spirit working with me, or am I resisting the Spirit?*

President David O. McKay used to counsel the Latter-day Saints to "sit down and commune with yourself. There is a battle going on within you, and within me, every day. Fight it out with yourself, and decide upon your course of action. . . . Decide where your duty is, . . . remembering that 'the greatest battle of life is fought out within the silent chambers of your own soul'" (Conference Report, April 1969, 95).

No other person on earth has access to our secret life, because "there is none else save God that knowest thy thoughts and the intents of thy heart" (D&C 6:16). Thus we can totally control this inner life, and from it we can reprogram our private and public lives. We must conscientiously work to get into this life. But if we will do so, and if we'll invite the Lord's Spirit there, it is the place where our public and private lives can be completely rescripted. If we will inwardly choose Christ, he can plant in us his motives, desires, and capacities, because he has the power to "make all things new" (Revelation 21:5). We can choose him because he has chosen us.

The Testimony of Jesus

The celestial kingdom is made up of those who were valiant in the testimony of Jesus (see D&C 76:79). What is Jesus' testimony, and how can we be valiant in it? Of course, that phrase means that we should be faithful to Christ, but beyond this, there is an additional insight that will come in understanding the divine role of Christ set forth in the scriptures. In each role, he is testifying to us of *us*—that is, of our own intrinsic worth and divine potential. Here are some of his roles. Notice how, in each role, he is testifying to us of our worth and potential. He was the *volunteer* in the premortal council in heaven, saying, "Here am I, send me" (Abraham 3:27). He was the *creator* of all things (Colossians 1:16). He was *Jehovah* of the Old Testament. He became our *Savior* and *redeemer.* He was the *deliverer* who opened the doors to the spirit world after his death to proclaim liberty to the captives (see Isaiah 61:1). He was the latter-day *restorer.* He will be the millennial *king.* He will be the *judge* of all mankind.

What is the "testimony of Jesus" in these eight roles? Why does he do all of these things? What motivates him to devote his entire time, energy, and attention to teaching and blessing and lifting people, even sacrificing his own life for us? He places unlimited value on people because he knows that we are his brothers and sisters and that we have the potential to become like God, as he did. That is the testimony he bears to us in each of his divine roles throughout all eternity.

Now, think about this—as our Savior and redeemer, he is also our advocate, testifying to God the Father about us. Think again about the words that he uses: "Listen to him who is the advocate with the Father, who is pleading your cause before him—saying: Father, behold the sufferings and death of him who did no sin, in whom thou wast well pleased; behold the blood of thy Son which was shed, the blood of him whom thou gavest that thyself might be glorified; wherefore, Father, spare these my brethren that believe on my name, that they may come unto me and have everlasting life" (D&C 45:3–5).

Also think on this—he is our mediator, so he is in a continuous role every time we offer a prayer or are involved in an ordinance. Everything is done in the name of Jesus Christ. So what does it mean to be valiant in the testimony of Jesus? In one sense, it means to believe what he says about us, to believe in his belief in us. It is to believe and to act on that belief that through the power of the Atonement we truly have the celestial capacity to become like our Heavenly Father.

Many mothers in Zion feel overwhelmed, unappreciated, and even unworthy when "all they're doing is raising kids." Consider this eternal perspective offered by Sister Sheri Dew: "If the day comes when we are the only women on earth who find nobility and divinity in motherhood, so be it. For *mother* is the word that will define a righteous woman made perfect in the highest degree of the celestial kingdom, a woman who has qualified for eternal increase in posterity, wisdom, joy, and influence" ("Are We Not All Mothers?" *Ensign,* November 2001, 96).

Victory over Self

When we send a spacecraft to the moon and back, it burns more fuel in the first few seconds than during the entire remainder of its half-million-mile journey. Why? To reach outer space, it has to overcome both the *gravity* of the earth and the *atmosphere* that surrounds the earth. And in a sense, we must overcome the same two forces—the *gravity of habits* in our private lives and the *social pressures* we encounter in the atmosphere of our public lives—before we can fulfill our divine potential.

One of our missionaries was very moody and undisciplined when he first came to Ireland. He was lazy in his habits and had trouble controlling his appetite, and within a short time he put on a lot of weight. He also had trouble controlling his temper, so he frequently blew up at his companion. When I counseled with him about these things, he promised to do better, but he never kept these commitments very long.

Following an argument with his companion one day, he asked me to transfer him to another area. I realized that I had been working with this elder at the wrong level and that I needed to go back to day one, so I decided on a new approach. I knew he wasn't getting up at 5:55 each morning as he was supposed to, so I asked him to do that every morning for a full month. He said, "How does that relate to the problem I'm having with my companion? Besides, I don't know if I can do it." So I asked him, "Will you do it for a week?" He agreed.

When I asked him about it a week later, he had kept his promise and was obviously thrilled with his achievement. I commended him for his integrity, and we set a new goal for him to continue getting up on time and to study the missionary discussions every morning. Each time he kept a commitment, I congratulated him and helped him establish a higher one. He began getting up at 5:30 A.M. on his own initiative, he learned to overcome his temper and to concentrate on his missionary work, and he no longer had any relationship problems with his companions.

Eventually he acquired so much control over his appetites and passions that he truly consecrated himself to the Lord.

President McKay taught that "spirituality is the consciousness of victory over self, and of communion with the Infinite. Spirituality impels one to conquer difficulties and acquire more and more strength. To feel one's faculties unfolding and truth expanding the soul is one of life's sublimest experiences" (*Gospel Ideals,* 390). As this elder progressed in his "victory over self," he became one of the most powerful teachers in the mission and brought many people into the Church. He was called to serve in leadership positions, was highly respected by the other missionaries, and inspired many of them to greater levels of dedication and accomplishment.

As this elder and I were on our way to the airport at the end of his mission, I asked him, "What's the most important thing you learned during your mission?" He said, "Getting up at 5:30 in the morning. That's the hardest thing I ever did. It was so cold that I could see my breath in the air. I did it on my own, because my companion was still legally asleep and didn't know what I was doing. But after I learned to get up at 5:30, everything else was easy."

The fruit of the spiritually motivated private victory is a broken heart and a contrite spirit. And when we have a broken heart and a contrite spirit, we have no desire to judge people. We feel God's love, and we sense that we have infinite worth. We don't need to compare ourselves with other people, because we know that we (and they) are precious beyond any human calculation. Also, we aren't offended by other people. How could we be offended by someone when we ourselves have been forgiven so massive an offense against God? In other words, we recognize our dependence on the Savior and carry a constant sense of gratitude toward him.

The Transforming Power of the Restored Gospel

On my mission, I traveled all around England. For one period I was in Liverpool for several days. We held street meetings every day down at the docks where the ships come in and out. There is a sidewalk near the docks and a little park out in front, and people would walk on the sidewalk and sometimes sit on benches that were there for rest and relaxation. We found that a perfect place to hold street meetings. We would stand on a little folding chair and give our messages to the people as they walked by. Most of them wouldn't stop. They would look a little, perhaps pause or slow down a little, but they usually wouldn't stop. Occasionally people would stop for a few minutes and then move on.

One day we noticed an old man sitting on a bench, but he seemed pretty much out of earshot, so we didn't pay too much attention to him, but he kept sitting there day after day. We somewhat dismissed him as being interested because he seemed so old, and he didn't seem to take any initiative in coming to us. But after a few days I went up to him and asked if he would like to hear more about what we were teaching. He showed a great deal of interest and said he would. So we went to his home and taught him the discussions in rapid-fire order. He could not consume them fast enough. He was absolutely filled with the Spirit and with a desire to learn. My guess is that he was in his eighties, and he was failing fast, but he had a keen mind.

To the consternation of his family, this man was baptized within just a few days of having the discussions. And then in entirely new ways he spent all of his waking hours studying the gospel, reading as much as he possibly could, particularly the great works written by the Brethren as well as a constant study of the scriptures in relation to those works. I continued doing my work and then found out that he was going to have a meeting with his family to say good-bye to them prior to his passing, and he asked if I would return to be with him at that meeting. I returned to Liverpool and stood in the room where he had gathered all of his loved ones, his children and their spouses and a few grand-children. It was a small room, and the place was totally filled with people. He lay on his bed and told them the story of his conver-sion and of his strong belief in the gospel as restored through the Prophet Joseph. Then he became very sober and precise in his language and said, "I know that you think I have lost my sanity and gone on in this newfound American religion, but I want to testify to you that it is the true gospel of Jesus Christ that has been restored to the earth, and you know how much I love you and care for you, and I am only interested in your welfare and happi-ness. You also know me to be an honest person. I want each of you to commit that you will allow the elders to teach you the story of the Restoration so that you will have an opportunity to understand what I have come to understand, what God has done for the salvation of his children in our day."

He looked at every person in the room and slowly received a positive nod from everyone that they would do this. Then he expressed his love and his testimony one more time and then said to them, "I am now going to move on into the spirit world, and I want you to know just how much I love you. Even though I am sad to say good-bye, I am happy to go to my God." Then he laid his head back on his bed, closed his eyes, and sang all of the verses to the hymn "Sweet Is the Work," at the conclusion of which he passed on. At the time I didn't interpret that experience through the six events, but since then I have thought back on it and see it as a perfect illustra-tion of them. He gained an understanding of God and himself, of Christ and his plan, he covenanted, he received the Holy Ghost and became a member of the Church, and then his consciousness started to move out toward all of his loved ones for their eternal welfare. He was only in the Church in mortality for a few months, but undoubtedly he is doing work on the other side, including work for his loved ones in the past and for generations to come, all of which is made possible through the atonement of Jesus Christ.

Taking the Initiative

As I've studied the six transcendent events of the Restoration, I've been deeply impressed by the fact that each one came about through the initiative of the Prophet Joseph Smith. Not only did he open the heavens by earnestly searching and praying to know the Lord's will, but he also fully carried out the Lord's instructions through a lifetime of constant effort. He became the instrument of restoring the gospel by translating the Book of Mormon and publishing it to the world. After being ordained to the apostleship in 1829, he took the initiative to reestablish the church and kingdom of God. He received and published many other revelations, "sent the fulness of the everlasting gospel . . . to the four quarters of the earth" (D&C 135:3), gathered thousands of converts, built cities and temples, restored the ordinances of the Lord's house, and instructed and organized the Saints to bring salvation to God's children on both sides of the veil. He did all of this in the face of severe persecution, demonstrating almost superhuman faith and courage, and finally he "sealed his mission and his works with his own blood" (ibid.).

By contrast, I believe that too many people simply wait for things to happen to them. For example, some have developed such bitter feelings about the deep, profound problems in their lives that they've become caught up in blaming and transferring responsibility. In many cases they're expecting God to take the initiative in solving their problems. But even though our difficulties can all be transcended through the power of the Atonement, we are the ones who must take the initiative to tap into that power.

President David O. McKay often taught that God, unlike Satan, allows us to take the initiative in our relationship with him. Why? Because he wants to promote the growth of his children. In fact, our personal development is the criterion for everything he does. Joseph Smith said that "God himself, finding he was in the midst of spirits and glory, because he was more intelligent, saw proper to institute laws whereby the rest could have a privilege to advance like himself. The relationship we have with God places us in a situation to advance in knowledge. He has power to institute laws to instruct the weaker intelligences, that they may be exalted with himself, so that they might have one glory upon another, and all that knowledge, power, glory, and intelligence, which is requisite in order to save them in the world of spirits" (*Teachings of the Prophet Joseph Smith*, 354).

The Savior said, "Ask, and it shall be given you; seek, and ye shall find; knock, and it shall be opened unto you" (Matthew 7:7). Ask, seek, knock—these are initiative words, and they tell us that we should become people who make things happen instead of passively waiting for things to happen. In fact, it is our very nature to do so. The scriptures say that through Christ's redemption "the children of men . . . have become free forever, knowing good from evil; *to act for themselves and not to be acted upon*" (2 Nephi 2:26; emphasis added).

Many people believe they can never really change because "this is just the way I am." In other words, they blame their nature. "I'm a night person, so don't talk to me in the morning. I'm always grumpy in the morning." "I'm not well organized." "I'm not as good as other people." And so forth. This kind of self-defeating determinism is part of the apostasy. It really is. The world's paradigms teach determinism; they teach us that we are victims of cultural forces and institutions. Thus many people just capitulate and literally wait for things to happen to them. But Joseph Smith's example teaches us that accepting responsibility for our lives is essential to our growth.

Become a person who takes the initiative and makes things happen. If you have difficulty in your marriage, it takes only one to make a difference—not two. Just start being a light instead of a judge. Start making deposits in the emotional bank account. Serve. Exercise kindness; keep the promises you make; be loyal; don't find fault. And when you make a mistake, apologize: "That was wrong. I'm sorry. I hope you can forgive me." Do these things for thirty days and see what begins to happen.

Taking initiative is especially crucial in our relationship with the Lord. If we want to bring about a personal restoration of the gospel in our lives—or in the lives of others—we must exercise faith in Christ and act with great courage, as Joseph Smith did. He once said, "God hath not revealed anything to Joseph, but what He will make known unto the Twelve, and even the least Saint may know all things as fast as he is able to bear them" (*Teachings of the Prophet Joseph Smith*, 149).

I believe that we have an enormous capacity to do good and to contribute to the world. I don't believe in a simple life. I believe in simple motivations, but I believe in a complex life filled with projects that can help other people. The Lord has instructed us that "men should be anxiously engaged in a good cause, and do many things of their own free will, and bring to pass much righteousness; for the power is in them, wherein they are agents unto themselves. And inasmuch as men do good they shall in nowise lose their reward" (D&C 58:27–28). I'm also convinced that this power within us, the power to do good, is greatly magnified and enhanced by our partnership with Christ. "For the works which ye have seen me do that shall ye also do. . . . Therefore, what manner of men ought ye to be? Verily I say unto you, even as I am" (3 Nephi 27:21, 27).

"Praise to the Man"

There are any number of positive qualities that the Prophet Joseph Smith demonstrated throughout his life, but I would particularly like to highlight four of them: faith in God and Christ, initiative, courage, and cheerfulness. These are four qualities that all of us can emulate. Let's look at each a little more closely.

First, *faith* in God and in his Son, Jesus Christ. This is the first principle of the gospel, the divine center of our lives. As you study each of the six events, you will find that faith was the driving principle behind them all. Starting with the First Vision, Joseph Smith was raised with and cultivated faith in God. When he read James 1:5, it stirred him so deeply that he could not help but act upon the promptings he received. You can practically *feel* his faith as you read his story.

Second, *initiative.* As mentioned earlier, as you study the six events, you will find that in every instance, without exception, Joseph Smith took the initiative. He acted; he was not acted upon. He prayed, he sought, he knocked, he asked. This initiative pattern and practice is overwhelming to me and motivates me to not wait to be told but rather to be anxiously engaged in many things that contribute to the building up of the kingdom. It teaches me we have enormous capacity, infinitely larger than the social mirror or software or self-doubts would counsel.

Third, *courage.* President Harold B. Lee taught, "Courage is the quality of every virtue acting at its highest testing point" (*Teachings of Harold B. Lee,* 606). Joseph Smith continually had to deal with his highest testing point. With few exceptions, he came through. In fact, after yielding to the persuasions of men and losing 116 translated pages of the Book of Mormon, he said, "I made this my rule: When God commands, do it." (*History of the Church,* 2:170.) His whole life was swimming upstream against powerful cultural and satanic forces. He was truly driven from pillar to post. He lost several children. He was beaten. He was tarred and feathered. He was continuously on the run, like a fugitive. He was imprisoned in a place ironically called "Liberty Jail." He suffered a martyr's death, knowing that he was going to that death like a lamb to the slaughter with a conscience void of offense to man or God. (See D&C 135:4.)

Fourth, *cheerfulness.* Joseph Smith always had a cheerful countenance and an uplifting, optimistic spirit about him. Try to imagine the burdens and responsibilities put on his shoulders and the difficulties, persecutions, constant setbacks, and almost insurmountable challenges he faced, not just occasionally but almost daily. Yet he was known as a cheerful, convivial spirit by all who encountered him.

I am convinced the reason he could be so cheerful in spite of all of his challenges was because he taught that faith and worry cannot exist in the same mind at the same time. To use the modern expression, he "let go and let God." He had a true peace about how God was using him and would continue to use him regardless of the difficulties he constantly confronted.

You can see how these four qualities are so intertwined: faith in God, initiative, courage, and cheerfulness. They are interdependent—they need each other for any one of them to work well. They are the fruits of being centered on God and Christ and seeing everything else as a stewardship. They come from looking through this gospel-centered lens at everything, at everybody, at every problem of the present, every concern about the future.

Two years before his death, Joseph Smith wrote, "The

Standard of Truth has been erected; no unhallowed hand can stop the work from progressing; persecutions may rage, mobs may combine, armies may assemble, calumny may defame, but the truth of God will go forth boldly, nobly, and independent, till it has penetrated every continent, visited every clime, swept every country, and sounded in every ear, till the purposes of God shall be accomplished, and the Great Jehovah shall say the work is done" (*History of the Church,* 4:540). This divine mission now rests upon the Latter-day Saints, and we have a sacred duty to bring God's light and truth to our family members and others.

I know that the Father and the Son appeared to Joseph Smith and worked through him to bring about the opening events of the latter-day Restoration. I know that the Book of Mormon contains the fullness of the gospel. I know that the Lord has restored the priesthood, his church, the keys of salvation, and the ordinances of the holy temple in our dispensation. I'm profoundly grateful for the diligence and the courage of the Prophet Joseph, who cheerfully suffered imprisonment and even martyrdom to accomplish the Lord's purposes. When I think about what he has done for all of us, it makes me want to sing, "Praise to the man who communed with Jehovah!" ("Praise to the Man," *Hymns,* no. 27).

The following words of testimony from Elder Bruce R. McConkie mirror my own feelings exactly:

> We need not fear for the future. This is the Lord's work; it is his kingdom; and he governs its affairs as he chooses. The keys, having been committed to man on earth, are now vested in those of his own choosing.
>
> And as the Lord lives, and as Christ is true, and as truth will prevail, I testify that this work shall roll forward until it fills the whole earth, and until the knowledge of God covers the earth as the waters cover the sea.

Now, this testimony I bear for myself and for all the faithful elders of the kingdom, and for all the sainted sisters who stand so valiantly at their sides, and above all I do it in the sacred and holy name of the Lord Jesus Christ. Even so, amen ("The Keys of the Kingdom," *Ensign,* May 1983, 23).

To Elder McConkie's testimony I add my own witness. I know that Jesus Christ is the Savior and Redeemer of the world, the light and the life of all mankind. He is our advocate and our mediator; he represents us and pleads our cause before our Heavenly Father. To remain perfect in Christ and grow toward his divine nature, we must "always remember him" (D&C 20:77, 79). We must repent and forgive. We must love as the Lord loves and not take offense. We must stay faithful and cheerful and loving toward all people.

We are engaged in a holy work, and we must not become discouraged or impatient with ourselves. If we have difficulty, let us go back to the first three events and become centered again. Through deep prayer and study and repentance, and through covenant-making at the sacrament table every Sabbath day, we will be renewed by the Spirit so that we continually return to the gospel path and become more and more like our Savior. And as we are integrated into the celestial culture through Christ-like service in our homes, in the Church, and in the temple, we will establish Zion, a people whom God can use to bless his children on both sides of the veil.

Willard Richards was a close friend and disciple of the Prophet Joseph Smith. He voluntarily accompanied the Prophet's brother Hyrum and John Taylor to the Carthage Jail. He declared his willingness, if the Prophet was condemned to death, to take his place. The Prophet asked Willard if he would accompany him into a room that was supposed to be safer.

Willard responded, "You did not ask me to cross the river with you—you did not ask me to come to Carthage—you did not ask me to come to jail with you—and do you think I would forsake you now? But I will tell you what I will do; if you are condemned to be hung for treason, I will be hung in your stead, and you shall go free" ("They Served," *Ensign*, January 1980, 26). Moments later, the mob entered the jail and killed the Prophet but miraculously failed to injure Willard Richards. Willard was a witness to the martyrdom of Joseph and Hyrum, giving divine force to their testimony, and he was a calming, peacemaking influence after the terrible tragedy.

Willard Richards was my Grandfather Richards's grandfather. When I was a young man, prior to my first mission to Great Britain, my grandfather told me that when he was a little boy, his grandfather, Willard Richards, bore testimony to him of the divine mission of Joseph Smith as God's restoring prophet. I remember him adding the words, "I know he did not lie. He told the truth."

My grandfather then bore his testimony to me of Joseph Smith, God's restoring prophet. Independent of their testimonies, I know he told the truth. I know it.

I believe that Willard Richards's consecrated testimony and life has blessed his posterity through their faithfulness in ways most of us are unaware of.

I express my love to all who read this book. I believe in Christ's testimony of you—that you are a literal son or daughter of God with infinite worth and potential, and that you have a significant, entirely unique mission in life and eternity. I testify that as we pay the price to have the gospel restored to us every day, we will gain greater hope in Christ and gradually become more like Him and our Father in Heaven.

BIBLIOGRAPHY

Benson, Ezra Taft. *The Teachings of Ezra Taft Benson.* Salt Lake City: Bookcraft, 1988.

Hafen, Bruce C. *The Broken Heart.* Salt Lake City: Deseret Book, 1989.

Holland, Jeffrey R. *However Long and Hard the Road.* Salt Lake City: Deseret Book, 1985.

Hymns of The Church of Jesus Christ of Latter-day Saints. Salt Lake City: The Church of Jesus Christ of Latter-day Saints, 1985.

Kimball, Spencer W. *Faith Precedes the Miracle.* Salt Lake City: Deseret Book, 1972.

———. *The Teachings of Spencer W. Kimball.* Edited by Edward L. Kimball. Salt Lake City: Bookcraft, 1982.

Lee, Harold B. *Stand Ye in Holy Places.* Salt Lake City: Deseret Book, 1974.

———. *Teachings of Harold B. Lee.* Edited by Clyde J. Williams. Salt Lake City: Bookcraft, 1996.

Lewis, C. S. *Mere Christianity.* New York: Macmillan, 1976.

McKay, David O. *Gospel Ideals: Selections from the Discourses of David O. McKay.* Salt Lake City: Improvement Era, 1953.

Petersen, Mark E. *The Great Prologue.* Salt Lake City: Deseret Book, 1975.

Pratt, Parley P. *Key to the Science of Theology/A Voice of Warning.* Salt Lake City: Deseret Book, 1965.

Smith, Joseph. *History of The Church of Jesus Christ of Latter-day Saints.* 7 vols. 2d ed. rev. Edited by B. H. Roberts. Salt Lake City: The Church of Jesus Christ of Latter-day Saints, 1932–51.

———. *Lectures on Faith.* Salt Lake City: Deseret Book, 1985.

———. *Teachings of the Prophet Joseph Smith.* Selected and arranged by Joseph Fielding Smith. Salt Lake City: Deseret Book, 1976.

Smith, Joseph F. *Gospel Doctrine: Selections from the Sermons and Writings of Joseph F. Smith.* Compiled by John A. Widtsoe. Salt Lake City: Deseret Book, 1939.

Smith, Joseph Fielding. *Doctrines of Salvation: Sermons and Writings of Joseph Fielding Smith.* 3 vols. Compiled by Bruce R. McConkie. Salt Lake City: Bookcraft, 1954–56.

Speeches of the Year, 1965. Provo: Brigham Young University Press, 1966.

Young, Brigham. *Discourses of Brigham Young.* Selected and arranged by John A. Widtsoe. Salt Lake City: Deseret Book, 1954.

PROBLEM/
OPPORTUNITY INDEX

This index is designed to be a resource in using the concepts and suggestions in *6 Events*. Use it to find answers about how you can implement these concepts and suggestions in your life.

THE LORD'S PROBLEM-SOLVING MODEL

What models can I look to for help in solving my problems?   6–7

How can I help myself and others to change?   8–11

How can I get the most from this book?   28–31

THE FIRST EVENT: THE FIRST VISION

Who? Who is God? Who is Christ? Who am I? Who are you?

How can I improve my understanding and concept
of myself?   45–49

What is my potential?   46

How can I better affirm the worth of myself
and others?   49–50, 58–66

How can I better understand my true nature?   49–52

How can I better understand and believe in the abundance
available in life?   52–58

How can I better affirm the members of my family?   66–69

How can I make my prayers more effective?   69–71

THE SECOND EVENT: THE RESTORATION OF THE GOSPEL

**Whose? Whose are we? To whom do we belong? Who paid the
price? Who is the source of our salvation?**

How can anyone in this life be perfect?   77–86

How can I become a better person?   77–86

How can I better deal with the imperfections of others?   87–91

What sacrifices does the Lord expect of me?   91–93

How can I repair a damaged relationship?   94–96

How can I keep from judging others?   97–99

How can I forgive others?   99–100

How can I have more empathy for others?   100

How can I be more like the Savior?   101–3

How can I better appreciate the Atonement?   103–6

THE THIRD EVENT: THE RESTORATION
OF THE PRIESTHOOD

**How? How do I get back to my God, my Father, my Creator? How
can I become a partaker of the divine nature?**

How can I better make and keep covenants?   113–16

How can I better take advantage of the power of the
priesthood?   116–18

How can I be "born again"?   118–19

How can I more fully appreciate the sacrament?   120–22

How can I better use the gift of the Holy Ghost?   122–31

What part of the gospel should I focus on right now?   131–32

THE FOURTH EVENT: THE RESTORATION
OF THE CHURCH

Where? Where do I go? Where can I find support, opportunity to serve, and direction for my life?

How can I better appreciate my Church membership?   138–39

How can my Church membership help me to
serve the Lord?   139–40

What can my Church membership do for me personally?   140–45

How can I strengthen my testimony of the gospel?   145

How can I stay active in the Church?   145–47

How can I be a better Church leader?   147–50

How can I better serve in the Church?   147–50

How can I strengthen others in the Church?   150–57

How can I broaden my influence for good?   157–59

THE FIFTH EVENT: THE RESTORATION OF
THE KEYS OF SALVATION

What? What do I do? What is my work in mortality?

How can I stop comparing myself with others?   52–58, 183–85

What is my part in the gathering of Israel?   165–71, 173–77

How can I receive the blessings I desire?   171–73

What is the most important Church work I can do?   177–82

How long should I serve?   182–83

THE SIXTH EVENT: THE RESTORATION OF
THE TEMPLE ORDINANCES

Why? What's it all about? Why am I on earth? Why do I need to be married for time and eternity?

How can I feel more connected with other people, including
my family?   190–93

What can I learn from my family?   193–94

How can I nurture my intergenerational family?   194–96

How can I get more out of attending the temple?   196–98

How can I better prepare to attend the temple?   198–203

How can I receive personal revelation?   203–7

How can I have more influence with others?   208–10

THE PERSONAL RESTORATION

When? The seventh question is answered in the sequence of the six events.

Where should I put my focus?   239–43

What should I do today?   247–51

How can I fulfill my potential?   252–54

How can I make things happen?   257–60

INDEX

Abraham, gospel of, 166–67
Abundance, versus scarcity, 52–58
Abuse, stopping cycle of, 194–96
Acceptance, of Atonement, 78–81
Action: internalizing and taking, 27–32; two levels of initiative and, 30–32
Advantage, definition of, 78
Advocate, Jesus Christ as, 82–86, 252
Affirmation, 60–62; of families, 66–69
AIDS, service and, 68–69
America: discovery of, 40–41; importance of, in Lord's work, 41–42; independence and Constitution of, 42–43
Apologizing, as sacrifice, 94–96
Apostasy: Restoration as response to, 7–8; sequence in bringing world out of, 224–25
Articles of Faith, sequence and, 229

Athletics, competition and scarcity mentality and, 54–55
Atonement: Orson F. Whitney's poem on, xiii–xiv; belonging to Lord through, 76; taking advantage of, 78–81; grace and works and, 89–91; receiving, through sacrifice, 91–93; as source of unity, 103; priesthood ordinances and, 111–13; order and, 139–40
Attitude: changing, 10; foster child changes, 46–47; understanding true identity leads to change in, 56–58; forgiveness and, 85–86

Balance, Boyd K. Packer on finding, 242–43
Ballard, M. Russell, on church and family, 177
Bamboo, conversion compared to, 231–32
Baptism: of Joseph Smith and Oliver Cowdery, 111; as

covenant, 114–15; as second birth, 118–19; perceiving change after, 128–29; keys of salvation and, 165

Basic needs, missionary work and, 64

Behavior: changing, 8–11, 96–97; foster child changes, 46–47; repairing relationships damaged by our, 94–96; culture as influence on, 201–2

Benson, Ezra Taft: on Constitution, 42, 43; on change through Christ, 229–30; on need for constant nourishment, 247

Birth, second, 118–19

Blessing, enemies, 82–86

Bloodletting, paradigm shift and, 9

Bodies, understanding and having respect for, 51–52

Book of Mormon: role of, in Restoration, 17; restoration of gospel through, as second event, 18, 103–4; Joseph Smith prays and receives, 75; faith as theme of, 76; ordinances and covenants and, 114

Branding, abusing bodies by, 51–52

Brigham Young University students, self-perception and, 58–59

Burdens, Atonement and, 91–93

Business, application of Lord's pattern in, 24

Calling: as opportunity to serve, 141–42; as means for growth, 142–43, 153–54; of Eli H. Pierce, to mission, 154–57; family as, 177–80

Cancer(s): author's sister and,

88–89; woman treated for, 117–18; five, 183

Categorizing people, 94–95

Change: adjusting to, 145–47; sequence of, 225; taking initiative to, 258–59

Charity, 54; C. S. Lewis on sins against, 184

Cheerfulness, of Joseph Smith, 261

Child of God, woman impressed to tell ward member she is, 124–26

Children: misbehaving, in subway, 10–11; affirming, 66–69; apologizing to, 95–96; Boyd K. Packer on raising, in unstable world, 176–77; as church callings, 178–80; sequence of teaching, 230. See also Commission on Children at Risk

Children of God, 49–52; high school teacher sees students as, 60–62. See also Identity

Church of Jesus Christ of Latter-day Saints, The: restoration of, as fourth event, 18, 135–59; serving, 20; establishment of, 135; evidence of truth and strength of, 136–37; institutionalizes gospel, 137–38; support system of, 138–39; as Lord's work, 139–40; as growth opportunity, 140–45; being centered in Christ, not in, 145–47; threefold mission of, 173–77, 183–85; Boyd K. Packer compares piano to, 242–43; Joseph Smith on expansion of, 261–62

Clark, J. Reuben, Jr., on serving Lord, 142

Columbus, Christopher, 40–41

Comfort zone, being outside our, 142–44, 157

Commandments: general and personal, 122–26; Harold B. Lee on most important, 131; establishment of Church of Jesus Christ and, 135

Commission on Children at Risk, 192–93

Commitments, making and keeping, 115–16

Common interests, finding, with people, 66

Communities: working in, as form of service, 157–59; importance of being active in, 174–75; as solution to social problems, 192–93

Comparisons, basing self-worth on, 52–54

Compass, restored gospel as, 21–24

Competition: self-worth and, 52–54; fifth event and, 183–85

Confession, acceptance of, 96–97

Connectedness, need for, 192–93

Connection, finding, with people, 66

Constitution, 70; Lord's hand in, 42–43; and Declaration of Independence, 136

Conversion, sequence of, 230–33

Courage: Harold B. Lee on, 260; of Joseph Smith, 260–61

Covenants: attaining perfection through, 77–78; eternal life and, 87; making, 113–16; Holy Ghost and making, 118–20; sacrament as means of renewing, 120–22; recommitting to, 146–47

Cowdery, Oliver: baptism of, 111; speaks with Christ in Kirtland Temple, 163–65

Creator, Jesus Christ as, 251

Culture: effect of, on faithfulness, 157–59; definition of, 201–2

Cycle, learn–commit–do, 31–32

Dark Ages, 7–8, 37–38; Bruce R. McConkie on, 7; Gordon B. Hinckley on, 38

Darkness, Restoration as response to, 7–8

Deacons, learn to appreciate fast offerings, 151

Dead, redeeming, 171

Death: of author's sister, 88–89; old man bears testimony before, 255–57

Deliverer, Jesus Christ as, 251

Determination, Ella Wheeler Wilcox on, xiii

Development, personal, 140–45

Dew, Sheri: on understanding who we are, 50–51; on mothers, 252

Diet, young woman starts, 79–81

Direction, to accomplish Lord's work, 139–40

Discovery, of New World, 40–41, 70

Divine mirror, 58–66

Divine potential, achieving, 252–57

Divine self-definition, 49–52

Divorce, 56

Doctors, impressed to treat cancer patient, 117–18

Dream: of lost little boy, 169–71; of grandfather and lost names, 171–73

Dysfunctional families, 194–96

Earth, as center of universe, 9

Edwards, Jonathan, on importance

of America in Lord's work,
41–42

Einstein, Albert, on paradigm
shifts, 9

Elijah: restoration of sealing power
and, 167–73; return of, 232–33

Empathy, 100

Endowment: missionaries learn to
appreciate, 196–98; Spencer W.
Kimball on preparing for,
198–99

Enduring, to the end, 182–83

Enemies, blessing, 82–86

Enlightenment, 69–70; as event
leading to First Vision, 40;
Jeffrey R. Holland on, 41

Especially for Youth, 51–52

Eternal families, 168–69; made in
temples, 190–93; relationships
in, 193–96

Eternal life, promise of, 87–91

Eternal marriage, 21

Eulogies, 88–89

Events, Restoration divided into
six, 18–19

Exaltation, definition of, 191

Examples, Christ, temple, and
Restoration as, 10

Expectations, living up to, 94–95

Fairness, as universal principle,
xii–xv

Faith: journal, 70–71; praying
with, 70–71; as theme of Book
of Mormon, 76; effect of
culture on, 157–59; to the end,
182–83; of Joseph Smith, 260

Families: affirming, 66–69; as
training center for missionaries,
152; eternal, 168–69, 190–96;
dysfunctional, 194–96

Family: prayer, 166; providing for,
175–77; and church work,

177–80; becoming perfect like
Christ through, 180–82; as
trial, 181–82; Proclamation on,
191–92; as authoritative
community, 193–96;
multigenerational, 194–96

Farthing, uttermost, 94–96

Fasting: as sacrifice, 92–93;
missionary has problem with,
241–42

Fast offerings, deacons learn to
appreciate, 151

Father: misbehaving children in
subway and, 10–11; learns he is
child of God, 67–68; stopping
sins of, 194–96

Fault-finding, 96–100

Faust, James E., on gift of Holy
Ghost, 130–31

Fellowshipping, 227–28

Fifth event, 163–85; restoration of
keys as, 18; internalizing,
183–85; temple and, 206

First event, 37–71; First Vision as,
18; internalizing, 69–71; temple
and, 206

First Vision, 37–71; as paradigm
shift, 11–12; as beginning of
Restoration, 15–16; as first
event, 18; self-identity and, 19;
events leading to, 39–44;
significance of, 44–45

Five cancers, 183

Forgiveness: asking for others',
94–96; foregoing judgment
through, 99–100; love and,
100. See also Atonement

Foster child, 46–47

Foundation, Christ as, 228–29

Fourth event, 135–59

Freedom, religious, 41–42

Fruit basket, 144–45

Funerals, 88–89

Gathering, 165–66

Germs, paradigm shift and, 9

Glory of God, focusing on, 88–89

Goals, reaching divine potential through, 253–54

Godliness, power of, 119–20

Goethe, Johanne von, on seeing people's potential, 150–51

Gospel: restoration of, as example, 6–7; restoration of, through Book of Mormon as second event, 18; restored, as compass, 21–24; events leading to restoration of, 43–44; restoration of, 75–107; defining, 76–77; as base of Church of Jesus Christ, 137–38; as Lord's work, 139–40; of Abraham, 166–67; being active in, 226; Boyd K. Packer compares piano to, 242–43. *See also* Restoration

Gossip, 54

Grace, works and, 89–91

Grandfather, dream of, searching for lost names, 171–73

Gratitude, 81–82

Great Awakening: first, 41, 69–70; second, 44, 70

Growth: advantage and, 78; personal, 140–45; callings as means for, 153–54

Guide, Holy Ghost as, 131–32

Guilt, man converted after feeling, 83

Hafen, Bruce C., on accomplishment of atoning sacrifice, 91

Healing: Christ as source of, 91–93; through priesthood power, 117–18; of dying child, 156–57

Heavenly Father: walking in presence of, 212–13; Joseph Smith on our relationship with, 258

Henley, William Ernest, xiii–xiv

Higher level, helping Saints reach, 150–59

High school teacher, 60–62

Hinckley, Gordon B.: on Dark Ages and Restoration, 38; on Renaissance, 39–40; announces Perpetual Education Fund, 174; on priorities, 175

Holland, Jeffrey R.: on events leading to discovery of New World, 41; tells story of Eli H. Pierce, 154–57

Holy Ghost: receiving, 118–19, 122–26; effects of, 126–27; Joseph Smith on receiving, 128; Parley P. Pratt on gift of, 129–30; James E. Faust on gift of, 130–31; as guide, 131–32

Home, temple as model, 204–5

Honesty: keeping covenants and, 116; priesthood power and, 116–18

House of learning, temple as, 203–7

House of Lords, 210–12

How? 20

Hypocrisy, 96–100

Identity: Dark Ages and, 37–38; First Vision and learning true, 44–45; revelation of true, 48–52; learning true, leads to change in attitude, 56–58; teaching children their true, 66–69; father learns his true, 67–68. *See also* Children of God, Self-concept

Influencing people, 66

Initiative: two levels of, 30–32; taking, 257–60; of Joseph Smith, 260

Institutionalizing, definition of, 135–36

Integrity: as universal principle, xii–xv; keeping covenants and, 116; priesthood power and, 116–18

Intelligence: relationship with God and, 52; in this life and spirit world, 78

Interdependency, 194

Internalizing, learning and, 27–32

"Invictus," xiii–xiv

Ireland: author's mission in, 104–6; missionaries reactivate Saints in, 239–41

Israel, keys of gathering of, 165–66

Jehovah, Jesus Christ as, 251

Jesus Christ: as example, 6; introduction of, 16; Book of Mormon and, 17; as Savior, 19–20; abundance mentality and, 55; faith in, as theme of Book of Mormon, 76; covenants with, 77–78; becoming perfect in, 77–82, 89–91; as rescuer, 81–82; as advocate, 82–86; as source of healing, 91–93; empathy of, 100; becoming perfect like, 101–3, 180–82; as mentor, 102; feasting on words of, 128–31; being centered in, 145–47; appears in Kirtland Temple, 163–65; as foundation, 228–29; Ezra Taft Benson on change through, 229–30; roles of, 251–52; testimony of, 251–52

Journal, faith, 70–71

Judge, Jesus Christ as, 251

Judging others, 96–100

Judgment, Joseph Smith on Lord's, 99

Justice paradigm, 89–91

Kant, Immanuel, on using understanding, 40

Keyboard, Boyd K. Packer compares gospel to, 242–43

Keys: restoration of, as fifth event, 18; restoration of, 20–21; of gathering of Israel, 165–66

Keys of salvation: restoration of, 163–85; Bruce R. McConkie on restoration of, 164–65

Kimball, Spencer W.: on Restoration, 15; on suffering and repentance, 100; on spiritual rebirth of Paul, 118–19; on restoration of sealing power, 168; on preparing for endowment, 198–99

Kindness, as universal principle, xii–xv

King, Jesus Christ as, 251

Kirtland Temple, dedication of, 163–65

Knowledge, in this life and spirit world, 78

Labeling people, 94–95

Leadership: of Church, 136–37; three models of, 147–50

Learn–commit–do cycle, 31–32

Learning: internalizing as part of, 27–32; teaching others as means of, 32; apostatizing and, 64–66; temple as house of, 203–7

Lee, Harold B.: on most important commandment, 131; on worthy living, 176; on church and home, 177; on importance of women in church work, 181; on courage, 260

Letter, from frustrated woman, 145–47

Lewis, C. S.: on pride, 55; on sins against charity, 184

Life: as mission, 182–83; public, private, and secret, 250–51

Lineage, of Joseph Smith, 43–44

Listening: understanding and, 63–64; prayer and, 70

Liverpool, England, conversion of old man in, 255–57

Lloyd, Elder, 208–9

London Temple: missionaries learn to appreciate endowment in, 196–98; trial on taxation of, 210–12

Lord's work, accomplishing, 139–40

Lost boy, dream of, 169–71

Love: unconditional, 60–66; showing, through sacrifice, 93; forgiveness and, 100; on author's mission, 104–6; need for, 138–39; of shepherd for sheep, 147–50; as principle taught in temple, 208–10; conversion and, 230–31; missionary learns to, 234–35

Madison, James, on Constitution, 42

Mamma Jackie, 68–69

Map, paradigm shift as, 9–11

Marriage: eternal, 21; temple ordinances as preparation for, 193–96; making changes in, 259

McConkie, Bruce R.: on Dark Ages, 7; on promise of eternal life, 87; on restoration of priesthood, 112–13; on restoration of keys, 164–65; testimony of, 262–63

McCracken, Judge, 232–33

McKay, David O.: on divine nature of man, 52; on spirituality, 174; on communing with self, 250; on taking initiative, 258

Mediator, Jesus Christ as, 252

Memories, Joseph F. Smith on premortal, 221–22

Mentalities, scarcity and abundance, 52–58

Mentor, Christ as, 102

Mercy paradigm, 89–91

Merrie Miss program, woman called to, 153–54

Miracles, priesthood power and, 117–18

Mirror, divine, 58–66

Mission: author's, in Ireland, 104–6; of Eli H. Pierce, 154–57; of Church of Jesus Christ, 173–77, 183–85; life as, 182–83; temples as integral part of, 199–200

Missionaries: faith journals and, 70–71; man accuses, 83; raising the bar for, 152; author challenged to increase number of, 157–59; learn to appreciate endowment, 196–98; reactivate Saints in Ireland, 239–41

Missionary: learns true identity, 49–50; learns to love, 62–63, 234–35; apostatizes, 64–66; learns Lord's plan for her, 206–7; teaches widow, 208–9; has problem with fasting, 241–42; learns self-control, 253–54

Missionary work: application of Lord's pattern in, 24; self-concept and, 47–49; gaining trust and, 59–60; dealing with basic needs as, 64; six events and, 222–23

Mistakes: three, in internalizing Restoration, 29–30; repenting of, 78–81

Model, 6–7; application of, 24; Jesus Christ as, 68; temple as, home, 204–5

Monson, Thomas S.: on taking action, 28; on deacons and fast offerings, 151

Mother: son prays for, 209–10; importance of, 252

Moyle, Henry D., 210–12

Nature, controlling, 116–17

Nauvoo Temple, importance of, 189–90

New World, discovery of, 40–41, 70

Offense, taking, 85–86

One-year project, 28–29

Order, to accomplish Lord's work, 139–40

Ordinances: of priesthood, 111–13, 119–20; priesthood covenants and, 113–16; restoration of temple, 189–215; as preparation for marriage, 193–96

Organizations: structures of, 135–36; support systems in, 138–39

Packer, Boyd K.: on doctrine and behavior, 8; on importance of stable home, 176–77; on

finding balance in Church, 242–43

Paradigm shift, 9–11

Parenting, 66–69; application of Lord's pattern in, 24

Parents, honoring, 194–96

Pattern: Restoration as, 7–8; application of, 24

Paul, Spencer W. Kimball on spiritual rebirth of, 118–19

Perfection: in Christ, 77–82, 89–91; of Christ compensating for weakness, 87–88; like Christ, 101–3; priesthood as path to, 119–20

Perpetual Education Fund, 174

Personal growth, 140–45

Personal revelation, in temple, 203–4

Petersen, Mark E., 197, 210–12

Piano, Boyd K. Packer compares gospel to, 242–43

Pierce, Eli H., mission of, 154–57

Plan, understanding Lord's, for us, 206–7

Plan of salvation, 168–69, 171

Play, life as three-act, 8–9

Potential: self-concept and, 46; Johanne von Goethe on seeing people's, 150–51; achieving divine, 157, 252–57; service as means to reach, 157–59

Power: of priesthood, 116–18; of godliness, 119–20

Pratt, Parley P., on gift of Holy Ghost, 129–30

Prayer: of Joseph Smith in Sacred Grove, 11–12; discovering true identity through, 49; internalizing first event through, 69; faith and, 70–71; sacrifice and, 92–93; importance of, 166; as principle learned in

temple, 210–12; renewing six
events and, 247–48

Pregnant woman, learns to
appreciate sacrament, 121

Preparation: of missionaries, 152;
for temple experience,
198–203, 228

Pride, C.S. Lewis on, 55

Priesthood: restoration of, as third
event, 18; restoration of, 20,
111–32; making, covenants,
113–16; power, 116–18; power
of godliness and, ordinances,
119–20; stewardship roles and,
157–59; restoration of sealing
power and, 168; three purposes
of, 173–77; heeding advice of,
leaders, 241–42

Principles, universal, xii–xv

Priorities, Gordon B. Hinckley on,
175

Private life, 250–51

Problems: Restoration as solution
to Lord's, 7–8; Atonement as
means to take away, 91–93;
blaming others for, 183–84

Proclamation on the Family,
191–92

Project, one-year, 28–29

Promise, eternal life as, 87–91

Promptings, woman feels, to call
ward member, 124–26

Public life, 250–51

Puritans, 41–42

Qualities, of Joseph Smith, 260–64

Questions, seven foundational,
19–21

Redeemer, Jesus Christ as, 251

Reformation, 69

Regional representative, author
attends prayer meeting as, 166

Relationship: building, with
Heavenly Father, 49; covenant,
77–78; Jesus Christ as advocate
in, 82–86; repairing, 94–96;
eternal family, 193–96

Religious freedom, 41–42

Renaissance, 69; as event leading to
First Vision, 39–40; Jeffrey R.
Holland on, 41

Renewal, need for, of six events,
247–66

Repentance, 78–81; sins against
others and, 83–84; true, 84–86,
96–100; paradigm, 89–91;
acceptance of, 96–97; suffering
and, 100

Rescuers, 81–82

Restoration: as example, 6–7; as
solution to Lord's problem,
7–8; of Church as fourth event,
18; of gospel through Book of
Mormon as second event, 18; of
keys as fifth event, 18; of
priesthood as third event, 18;
divided into six events, 18–19;
of temple ordinances as sixth
event, 18–19; of priesthood, 20,
111–32; of keys of salvation,
20–21, 163–85; of temple
ordinances, 21, 189–215; chart
summarizing six events of,
22–23; internalizing, 27–32;
three mistakes in internalizing,
29–30; Gordon B. Hinckley on,
38; events leading to, 43–44; of
gospel, 75–107; of Church,
135–59; Bruce R. McConkie
on, of keys of salvation,
164–65; of sealing power,
167–73; purpose of, 190–93;
definition of, 221

Restorer, Jesus Christ as, 251

Resurrection, knowledge in, 78

Retirement, 182–83

Revelation: true identity and, 48–49; personal, in temple, 203–4

Richards, Stephen L, 52, 210–12

Richards, Willard, testimony of, 263–64

Roles, of Christ, 251–52

Rushing, temple work and, 200–201

Sacrament, 81, 120–22; as chance to renew covenants, 114–15

Sacred, separation of secular and, 173–77

Sacred Grove, Joseph Smith prays in, 11–12. *See also* First Vision

Sacrifice: receiving Atonement through, 91–93; forgiveness and, 94–96; repenting sins as, 96–100; service and, 144–45; temple work as, 171; love and, 208–10

Salvation, 20–21; as current event, 81–82; grace and works and, 89–91; restoration of keys of, 163–85; plan of, 171

Savior, Jesus Christ as, 251

Scarcity, versus abundance, 52–58

Scott, Richard G., on stewardship, 152–53

Scriptures: ordinances and covenants and, 114; studying, after receiving Holy Ghost, 126–27; feasting on, 128–31

Sealing power, restoration of, 167–73

Second birth, 118–19; perceiving change after, 128–29

Second event, 75–107; restoration of gospel through Book of Mormon as, 18; internalizing, 103–7; temple and, 206

Secret life, 250–51

Secular, separation of sacred and, 173–77

Self-concept, social and divine, 45–49

Self-control, missionary learns, 253–54

Self-definition, divine, 49–52

Self-identity, 19

Self-perception, 58–66

Self-worth: basing our, on comparisons of others, 52–54; converted woman realizes, 56–58; teaching children, 66–69; and service, 68–69

Separation, of sacred and secular, 173–77

Sequence: of six events, 21–22; importance of, 29–30, 221–36; violating, 233–36

Service: as universal principle, xii–xv; self-worth and, 68–69; prayer and, 71; calling as, 141–42; as growth opportunity, 142–43; sacrifice and, 144–45; as means to reach potential, 157–59; love and, 208–10

Seven foundational questions, 19–21

Shepherd, sheepherder, and sheep, 147–50

Sins: against others, 83–84; giving away our, 96–100; against charity, 184

Sister, death of author's, 88–89

Six events: Restoration divided into, 18–19; sequence of, 21–22; chart summarizing, 22–23; temple embodies, 206; missionary work and, 222–23; importance of experiencing all, 239–43; need for constant renewal of, 247–66

Sixth event, 189–215; restoration of temple ordinances as, 18–19; temple and, 206; internalizing, 213–15

Smith, Joseph: First Vision as paradigm shift for, 11–12; on First Vision, 16; preparation of, 16–18; as example of internalizing, 27–28; lineage of, 43–44; on comprehending ourselves, 50; as model, 68; prays and receives Book of Mormon, 75; on being perfected in Christ, 77; on Lord's judgment, 99; on Book of Mormon, 103; baptism of, 111; on being born again and ordinances, 112; on priesthood power, 116–17; on receiving Holy Ghost, 128; speaks with Christ in Kirtland Temple, 163–65; importance of building temples and, 189–90; on love, 208; on understanding God, 225; initiative of, in restoration of gospel, 257; on our relationship with God, 258; qualities of, 260–64; on obeying God's commandments, 261; on expansion of Church, 261–62; Willard Richards's testimony of, 263–64

Smith, Joseph F., on premortal memories, 221–22

Smith, Joseph Fielding, on restoration of sealing power, 168

Sodom and Gomorrah, Boyd K. Packer on, 176–77

"Soul's Captain, The," xiii–xiv

Spirituality, David O. McKay on, 174

Spirit world, knowledge in, 78

Stake president: influences missionary, 64–66; woman forgives, 84–85

Stewardship: Richard G. Scott on, 152–53; callings and, 153–54

Structures, of organizations, 135–36

Students, teacher sees, as children of God, 60–62

Subway, misbehaving children in, 10–11

Suffering: Atonement as means to take away, 91–93; repentance and, 100

Support system, of Church, 138–39

Taxation, of London Temple, 210–12

Teacher: sees students as children of God, 60–62; son prays for, 209–10

Teaching: application of Lord's pattern in, 24; as means of learning, 32

Teenagers, affirming, 66–69

Temple: as example, 6; prayer meeting in, 166; work, 169–71; significance of, 190–93; as Lord's university, 196–98; preparation for going to, 198–203, 228; missionary service and, 199–200; culture of, 202–3; personal revelation in, 203–4; as house of learning, 203–7; as model home, 204–5; embodies six events, 206; principles taught in, 208–13

Temple ordinances: as sixth event, 18–19; restoration of, 21, 189–215

Temptation, resisting, 127

Testimony: of divine nature,

59–60; of Christ, 251–52; man
bears, before his death, 255–57;
of Bruce R. McConkie,
262–63; of author, 263; of
Williard Richards, 263–64
Third event, 111–32; restoration
of priesthood as, 18;
internalizing, 131–32; temple
and, 206
Three mistakes, in internalizing
Restoration, 29–30
Three purposes, of priesthood,
173–77
Tithing, as sacrifice, 92–93
Transcendent, definition of, 6–7
Trials: Atonement and, 91–93;
families as, 181–82; blaming
others for, 183–84
True north, 21–24
Trust, missionary work and
earning, 59–60
Truth, as accurate map, 10
Two levels of initiative, 30–32

Unconditional love, 60–66
Understanding: internalizing and,
27–32; Immanuel Kant on
using, 40; listening and, 63–64;
service and, 71
Unity, Atonement as source of, 103
Universal principles, xii–xv
University, temple as Lord's,
196–98
Uttermost farthing, 94–96

Victory, private and public,
249–51
Visitors, heavenly, during
Restoration, 16–18
Volunteer, Jesus Christ as, 251

Walking in presence of God,
212–13

Weakness: delighting in, of others,
52–54; focusing on our, 79–81;
Christ's perfection compensates
for, 87–88
Welfare, family and church,
175–77
What? 20–21
When? 21–22
Where? 20
Whitney, Orson F., xiii–xiv
Who? 19
Whose? 19–20
Why? 21
Widtsoe, John A., on Joseph
Smith's building temples, 190
Wilcox, Ella Wheeler, on
determination, xiii
Women, Harold B. Lee on church
work and, 181
Wooden, John, on competition, 55
Woodruff, Wilford, on Founding
Fathers, 43
Words of Christ, feasting on,
128–31
Work, church and family, 177–80
Worker, author builds relationship
with, 94–95
Works: grace and, 89–91;
priesthood ordinances and,
111–13

Young, Brigham: on knowing
ourselves, 50, 52–53
Young Women program, woman
called to, 153–54

Zion, definition of, 173–77